GO DEEP.
TAKE CHANCES.

Embracing the Muse & Creative Writing

Books by Roger Armbrust

How to Survive (poems)

Final Grace (brief book)

The Aesthetic Astronaut (sonnets)

oh, touch me there (love sonnets)

Go Deep. Take Chances. (writing guide)

Pressing Freedom (novel)

The Vital Realities for 2020 and Beyond (writings)

Viper's Reckoning (novel scheduled for 2021)

Maestro Love Sonnets (scheduled for 2020)

GO DEEP.
TAKE CHANCES.

Embracing the Muse & Creative Writing

Roger Armbrust

Parkhurst Brothers Publishers

MARION, MICHIGAN

www.parkhurstbrothers.com

Consumers may order Parkhurst Brothers books from their favorite online or bricks-and-mortar booksellers, expecting prompt delivery. Parkhurst Brothers books are distributed to the trade through the Chicago Distribution Center. Trade and library orders may be placed through Ingram Book Company, Baker & Taylor, Follett Library Resources and other book industry wholesalers. To order from Chicago Distribution Center, phone 1-800-621-2736 or fax to 800-621-8476. Copies of this and other Parkhurst Brothers Publishers titles are available to organizations and corporations for purchase in quantity by contacting Special Sales Department at our home office location, listed on our web site. Manuscript submission guidelines for this publishing company are available at our web site.

Printed in the United States of America

First Edition, February 2020

Printing history: 2020 2021 2022   10 9 8 7 6 5 4 3 2 1

Library of Congress Cataloging in Publication Data:
Names: Armbrust, Roger, 1943
Title: Go Deep. Take Chances: Embracing the muse and creative writing
Description: First Edition. Marion, Michigan: Parkhurst Brothers, 2019
Identifiers: ISBN 978-62491-090-6 Trade Paperback and
ISBN 978-1-62491-091-3 E-book
Subjects: LCSH: Authorship. Creation, Literary
English Language—Rhetoric
LCC PN149 .M43 2019 // DDC 808.02—dc23

ISBN: Trade Paperback   978162491-090-6
ISBN: e-book   978162491- 091-3

Cover design by   Linda D. Parkhurst
Interior design by   Susan Harring
Acquired for Parkhurst Brothers Publishers
And edited by: Ted Parkhurst

012020

To my daughter Catherine

my mentor, the late William Packard

my friend Ted Parkhurst

and all my loving assurances of support

introduction

One semester, my creative mentor William Packard asked me to teach his poetry-writing course at New York University's School of Continuing Education and Professional Studies. He did so because I had taken the course, he considered me a good poet, and knew I was teaching a professional-writing course of my own at NYU. Each time I'd walk in to instruct his poetry-writing class, I'd scratch on the chalkboard two brief sentences: *Go deep. Take chances.*

These two suggestions represent, I believe, the keys to creative writing. There exist keys to basic good writing, which I also will cover here, and which remain required of writers wishing to communicate clearly and concisely. But creative writing consists of steps and, yes, leaps which meld writer and reader in a way where they share, not just the experience of facts, feelings and imagination, but insight into existence.

To set the stage for our journey, I offer you a verbal map, a summary of my creative philosophy. It sprang forth, to my surprise, in 2004 within an e-mail to a friend of a friend who wanted feedback on her short story. This book will expand on points I made in that e-mail. I hope this effort will help you as you approach your own creative writing. It's a process we often face early-on with passion, drive, and fear of rejection. With this book, perhaps I can lead you to better understand and execute the process, bringing you serenity and satisfaction—maybe even joy and a sense of self—with the extremely focused work of creativity.

Here's the e-mail section dealing with creative philosophy which, of course, contains no new ideas; but it's what I've experienced, and what I believe:

It's important to know that—if you want to keep writing—this story doesn't stand alone. It's a part of the continuum of your creativity. The past writing you've done and the future writing you'll do. The fine photography you're currently involved in—another process using creative imagery. One helps expand the other.

Most of all, it's important to remember that what I, or anybody else thinks or feels, or how we respond to your creative work, doesn't really matter. What matters is the spiritual experience of your work—the continuing, changing and growing connection with the Great Spirit that is deep within you. That's why we do this.

Rainer Maria Rilke has said that, if we feel we MUST write, we should use our experience, our imagination, and our dreams. Really, that's all we have to go on. And that's all a reader or listener has to go on—his or her own experience, imagination and dreams. The reader's response will be based on that. We have no control over it, nor should we want to. Our job is to speak as honestly as we can at the moment, and have faith that the reader somehow identifies and grows, however minutely, by reading and experiencing our honest writing.

By honest, I don't mean it has to be factual. That's where the power of imagination and dream comes in. We use it all to create AN EXPERIENCE FOR THE READER. And that first reader is you, the writer.

If you want to read about writing, I'd suggest William Packard's <u>The Art of Poetry Writing</u> from St. Martin's Press. He speaks clearly about the power of imagery and sound and rhythm in writing, and a myriad other things that will help all writers, not just poets.

You might also take a look at Rilke's <u>Letters to a Young Poet</u>, 10 short letters he wrote which include wise words about the development of the artist. I recommend the translation by Herter-Norton.

Since you've been good enough to share some writing with me, I'll close with a sonnet that pretty well sums up my life view.

Bless,
Roger

THE HOLIEST LIGHT

Galileo, his telescope the new
extended eye mapping orbits of stars,
must have whispered to himself, "Dear sir, you
now, both scientist and poet, rise far
too close to heaven. What do you think popes
will say to this sacrilege? Rewrite Church
law for your sake? This curved glass is a rope
they'll use to noose your neck. But let my search
kill both me and their terrifying faith,
strangle their shouts with truth of heaven's face.
Let this universe, as one, form the lathe
which tools all fear into a sacred space
where we speak from hearts: the holiest light."
Our eyes traject our deepest love tonight.

table of contents

six basics of good writing

1. honesty – more than facts: the vital center of human relationship, including writer and reader.

2. general/specific – embracing writing's natural flow to caress the reader – the more specific, the clearer to the reader.

3. imagery/concrete nouns/active verbs – bringing solid reality to the reader's imagination – energizing writing and reader with living verbs.

4. metaphor/denotation/connotation – discovering similarities in dissimilar images – expanding the reader's consciousness through an image's specific meaning and its suggested meanings.

5. scrapping prepositions – tightening writing through turning a phrase into an active verb.

6. no absolute rules – after mastering basics, dancing with the Muse leads to new steps.

six suggestions to teachers – guiding young poets and writers (those young in the work).

go deep

After one of my professional-writing classes at NYU, a student came up to me and asked, "Why do you write?"

I responded, "Do you mean poetry, which I consider the most important writing that I do?"

"Well, yes."

"Because it's the closest thing I know to a spiritual experience."

She seemed a bit stunned by that, so I decided to put the statement in perspective.

"I didn't come up with that idea," I said, smiling. "Homer opens *The Odyssey* by saying, 'Sing to me of the man, Muse...' He's calling on this higher power to communicate to him and through him, that he may tell a wonderful story."

Indeed, the classical creators all seemed to understand the need to go deep, to tap into that conscious contact with a powerful resource both within and outside them. The Greeks and Romans called on a "Muse," one of the nine goddesses of poetry, song, the arts and sciences.

In the eighth or ninth century BC (depending on who you talk to) the Greek poet Homer, this time in *The Iliad*, opens with the prayer, "Rage—Goddess, sing the rage of Peleus' son Achilles..." Some 800 years later, the Roman poet Virgil entreats as he begins *The Aeneid*, "Tell me the reason, Muse..."

Now, move up to the wonderful Russian poet Anna Akhmatova early in the 20th century—this from her poem "The Muse":

> And she enters. Drawing aside her shawl
> She gazed attentively at me.
> I said to her: "Was it you who dictated to Dante
> The page of *The Inferno*?" She replied: "It was I."

With this poem, Akhmatova provides two powerful messages for anyone who wants to move toward creative artistry:

First, if you want to write, you connect with the Muse, the Ultimate Reality, the Great Spirit, the Higher Power, the Great Breather, the God of God, Light of Light, True God of True God, the Intelligent Essence, the Endless Energy—call it what you will. The artist's job is to link up with that great voice of the universe which seems to sing within us and around us.

Second, we pay attention to what great literature has gone before us. In the case of Akhmatova's persona in *The Muse*, she has witnessed this overwhelming force enter her room, toss back her shawl, and consider whether the young poet is ready for her. Akhmatova's persona wisely and humbly asks her awaited guest's identity by questioning whether her voice guided the Italian poet Dante through his literary masterpiece. And the Muse, always dedicated to brevity, provides her three-word answer, which in some translations from Russian to English becomes tightened to a single breath: "Yes."

So, there we have it. To thrive in the creative process, we call on the Great Voice of the Universe to sing through us, and we also make conscious contact with that voice by reading the great literature which sang before our writers' generation came into being.

How do you make that personal conscious contact with The Muse? That's up to you. I can only tell you how I do it. And that's basically the way Homer did it. I pray and listen. Not the prayer of any religion, except my personal religion of poetry, which fits within my belief of the great loving intelligent energy that creates and makes up all—stars and planets, air and earth, flesh and mind, birth and death, fear and destruction, faith and love. What do I pray for? Most of all, to be honest and open-minded. How else can I faithfully go deep? How else can I fearlessly take chances? How else can I risk finding out who I really am and what life really is? How else can I translate that into a literary experience for myself and any other reader?

When I look at myself in relation to history and the universe, the truth is, I'm not much. I don't know much, and I haven't experienced much. And yet, through this conscious contact, I begin to understand my place on earth, in history and the universe, and the unique essence within me and around me. That's where, it seems to me, creative reading and creative writing take us.

It's a deep place. And it can prove a fearful, frustrating trek if we try to go it alone. I've done that. I can tell you there's a marked contrast in, first, taking on the relentless creative drive by myself— feeling only I possessed these flaming emotions, dramatic longings of experience, fear of death and of rejection, and stalwart belief that my first draft was the true word laid before all—and, later, the focused creative conversation arising when I open to the Muse's caress.

My experience tells me that, when you let go to the Muse, you find it. Open-minded conscious contact leads you to great reading, intense observation and involvement in the world, honest (and therefore real) relationships, and a clear, loving, unshakeable voice in your writing.

William James says we reach this place through **faith** and **action**. By faith, he seems to mean an individual's personal relationship with the divine. That's basically how he described it in his book *The Varieties of Religious Experience*, based on his series of lectures which didn't deal so much with organized religions, but with individuals' personal spiritual encounters.

James, who was a medical doctor, psychologist, philosopher and teacher—and older brother of the novelist Henry James—believed in *concrete* spiritual experiences. That is: humans' spiritual experiences lead to psychic changes, which in turn lead to changes in the way they think, feel, speak, write and live.

The Columbia University professor Wayne Proudfoot places James' view of concrete spiritual experiences into five categories: "voices and visions, responses to prayer, changes of heart, deliverances from fear, and assurances of support."

I believe we experience all those when we're involved in the creative-writing process. And I know that process can clarify existence for us, and bring change to our lives, and even to others, whether we writers immediately realize it or not, and whether a reader expects it or not.

Nikola Tesla in 1870, at age 24, reciting aloud from Johann Wolfgang von Goethe's verse drama *Faust*, suddenly foresaw AC currents propelling induction motors—technology which didn't exist. His great idea would lead to electric power grids, and stun thousands at Chicago's World's Fair when he presented a "City of Light." His design eventually would shower the globe with energy and light, changing the way people worked and lived.

What were the specific lines that helped poetry shake science? Tesla, later called the Father of Physics, cited these:

> *The glow retreats, done is the day of toil;*
> *It yonder hastes, new fields of life exploring;*
> *Ah, that no wing can lift me from the soil*
> *Upon its track to follow, follow soaring!*

What does that tell you about the power of creative writing? The German Goethe, who died 24 years before Tesla's birth in the Balkans, probably didn't say to himself, "Well, I think I'll write *Faust*, and it will help Tesla scientifically change civilization." Knowing the creative process's power, including its psychic potential, he could have! And Goethe did perform research in the natural sciences. But the odds are, while expecting society's advancement, he probably didn't specifically foresee Tesla, or his own verse causing such a tremendous technological impact.

Can you see how the creative process not only ignites the writer's imagination, but the reader's? Writing's imagery and rhythms invite both creator and recipient to explore and expand their worlds, and can induce an endless flowering of understanding and growth. The creative connection between writer, Muse, and reader can, if one considers Tesla's experience, literally change the individual, and perhaps even the world.

Still, I believe this only can occur when writers trust the Muse and their own experience, imagination, and dreams, and don't concern themselves with how a reader might react. One might worry about that in some other writing form, such as business or governmental reports, but not in creative writing. Here, our job is to not limit ourselves, or restrict ourselves with any reader's limits. We write to grow, and invite any reader to grow also.

"I have only three criteria for what I go on reading and teaching: aesthetic splendor, intellectual power, wisdom," says Yale scholar and writer Harold Bloom in his book *Where Shall Wisdom Be Found?* "Societal pressures and journalistic fashions may obscure these standards for a time, but mere Period Pieces never endure. The mind always returns to its needs for beauty, truth and insight. Mortality hovers, and all of us learn the triumph of time."

With that in mind, isn't it best to use our limited time well? What better way than going deep and taking chances through the creative process?

MUSE OF FIRE

Anna understood about throwing
back her veil, her staring down any gaze.
Will knew each sonnet began with bowing
before her, staying bent until she raised
him up, steadied his hand holding the quill.
Homer would petition her sacred song
to flow through his creative being, fill
his voice with hypnotic rhythms. What's wrong
with my seeking her magic breath in this
age of endless war, surveillance taping
last gasps of free speech, death of new thought, kiss
of my parched lips on her sunken cheek? Sing
some Disney tune to an empty room. Curse
in whispers of despair, or something worse.

Roger Armbrust
June 30, 2013

continuum of our creativity

Our senses, intelligence, emotions and, (yes, William James!) faith and action are the library of our creative research and expression. They endlessly caress our conscious, subconscious, even unconscious selves.

Before birth, the brain's sight, the mother's heartbeat, the blood flow's pace already affect the future writer. Ancients from Abraham to Plato up to modern religions and writers have expressed belief that the process begins even before that: in pre-existence. Wordsworth and Yeats join that vast throng.

My experience tells me that, whenever it begins, creativity just keeps growing, as long as we're open to what our senses, intelligence, emotions, and faith and action bring us.

The poet Miller Williams, offering advice on writing, states it this way through his poem's title and opening:

Let Me Tell You

how to do it
from the beginning:
First, notice everything.

To a body-mind-spirit not used to such an activity as noticing everything, such advice may seem intimidating. But to the centered writer, Williams' offer has its reasonable limits, because our bodies and energies possess limits. So, on that level, we can only notice our immediate environment. But Williams and other poets know this: Our immediate environment is the concrete key that opens up the universe to us. The more intently we observe our place and its interconnections, the clearer our view and understanding of existence. This is because our mind and imagination begin reaching for those connections:

ACORN

Sometimes its cupule appears a sculpted
lampshade for a dollhouse, a basket weaved
of overlapped leaves—bracts armored and fed
by weathered ages—or locket conceived
to bear a minute goddess's perfect
breast. Look closely, love, inside this small shell:
how its round wall rises from white to flecked,
faded crimson; tricklings like bloodstains tell
of nature's endless birth. See the squirrel
on the oak branch there, breaking brown nut free
of its casing. How her sharp, sure claws twirl
and clasp the kernel, teeth knifing cleanly
to pale meat. Its smooth, moist substance heralds
a jewel: opal tinged with emerald.

Roger Armbrust
January 1, 2009

James Joyce, inviting the reader in to first sensations of life, keeps the sense description very simple: "When you wet the bed first it is warm then it gets cold." And while anyone who's studied literature might complain of Joyce's line being overused from high school to college, the truth remains: He's clear, concise, honest, and offers the reader the chance to experience, or even recall experience.

Each sense matters, though sight and sound seem to command imagery. Check out Thomas Wolfe in *Look Homeward Angel*:

… and when the mountain boy brings water to his kinsmen laying fence, and as the wind snakes through the grasses hears far in the valley below the long wail of the whistle, and the faint clangor of a bell; and the blue great cup of the hills seems closer, nearer, for he had heard an inarticulate promise…

We use our senses in every creative endeavor. Therefore, when melded with our sixth sense and memory, our potential for creative growth just might be limitless. We could argue our creativity ends when our body turns to dust or ash. But Yeats and others might argue:

But in the grave all, all, shall be renewed.
The certainty that I shall see that lady
Leaning or standing or walking
In the first loveliness of womanhood,
And with the fervour of my youthful eyes,
Has set me muttering like a fool.

This melding of senses and memory allows experience to translate into creativity. The Greeks loved memory, and it's no wonder. What good are we humans without it?

ALL THE ALL OF ME

When image comes, it consumes. When phrase coats
throat like melted chocolate, vinegar,
or acid, no choice remains but to float
to stunned keyboard, observe my gnarled fingers
begin their passionate yet timid dance.
Dark letters fill white space with stuttered pace:
slow step, brief lurch, sudden dash, nimble prance.
Phrase grows to line grows to column. This grace
of sight and sound, this tight list of reason
and illusion, this gathering of mist
and memory into days and seasons
of sacred chants proves how Erato kissed
Sappho's quill, how Calliope embraced
Homer as his dazed hands studied her face.

Roger Armbrust
May 28, 2013

take chances

My own understanding of faith and action as the key to creativity really solidified when I began to listen to William James. Here's a quote from a long James lecture-essay I've shared with many, from friends to students. The italics within also belong to James:

Not a victory is gained, not a deed of faithfulness or courage is done, except upon a maybe; not a service, not a sally of generosity; not a scientific exploration or experiment or textbook, that may not be a mistake. It is only by risking our persons from one hour to another that we live at all. And often enough our faith beforehand in an uncertified result *is the only thing that makes the result come true.*

The quote comes from James's lecture-essay "Is Life Worth Living," in which he eventually determines that it certainly is. I became aware of the essay when reading Laurence Thomson's definitive, Pulitzer Prize-winning biography of Robert Frost. I was extremely distraught at the time, having seen a dear love leave, feeling I was dealing with unbearable pain, and trying to find at least a salve if not salvation through others' written words.

I decided to pick up the biography I had earlier abandoned, went to my bookmark, and was startled to begin reading about Frost in his mid-twenties, obsessing with suicide. I identified with that obsession and was mesmerized to see that Frost had stumbled on to James's essay. It not only delivered him from a drive for self-destruction, it inspired him to return to college, which he had left as a promising but self-pitying freshman. He had stolen away from Dartmouth at 18, but now was determined to enter Harvard where James taught. Long story short, he convinced his wife Elinor, studied and passed the grueling entrance exams, and walked on to campus only to learn that James had taken a year's sabbatical. Best laid plans. But Frost had decided to grow rather than die, thanks to the written word.

I relate this story to you because poets and writers, in their processes of going deep and taking chances, may often become self-absorbed, experience fear, maybe even terror, and writer's block, especially in the early going. The only cure I know for that fear and self-absorption is the faith and action James speaks of, and finding that through a *personal* relationship with the divine that he espouses.

In writing, it's that faith that leads us to move forward, to leap, and, yes, to dance in our creative expression. And it doesn't necessarily have to be happy expression:

DEEP FREEZE

As I lie in bed, fears and obsessions
hurl like ice daggers through my brain, heart, gut
and penis, turning my being, my one
hope, to fragile frozen crust, delicate
equilibrium quivering to edge,
then avalanche, swirling me far within
the abyss. Dark drift of depression's ledge…
is it ledge…is it bottom…is it sin's
last step?...paralyzes even panic.
Encapsuled in blackness, somehow I know
my senses surround me, monoclinic
crystals crushing my furling psyche, slow
torture telling of what's to come. A frost
steals my breath, whispers, *Now your soul is lost.*

Roger Armbrust
January 10, 2009

Again, the writer's job is to express herself as honestly as possible to create an experience. We can become timid. Say to ourselves, "I can't write something depressing like that, or show it to anyone. What will people think? I might even depress them to the point they'll do something destructive." Well, yes, they might. But they might also read it and say, "I've felt exactly that way. I'm not alone. Thank God." And maybe even take a positive action. Here's the reality: We don't have control over others' experience, imagination, and dreams. But if we honestly relate ours or the persona's within the writing, and the reader honestly opens to it, that's where the connection occurs. And more often than not, when the human feels honest connection, even if it's painful, we can grow from it.

Walt Whitman understood this:

I celebrate myself, and sing myself,
And what I assume you shall assume,
For every atom belonging to me as good belongs to you.

It's tough to celebrate in this age of satellites and drone cameras and bombs, endless war, embedded chips, and government and corporate tracking of your phone calls, emails and other Internet activity. It can lead the fearful human soul to shut down its creative nature. But the concrete spiritual experiences James speaks of can enfold and fill the writer, enabling the artist to take chances.

I spoke earlier of Professor Proudfoot dividing James' concrete spiritual experiences into five categories. Here they are, and how I believe they relate to us in our creativity.

voices and visions

I have a young friend, a very good writer who would love to become a dedicated writer. When I spoke to him of James, and of voices and visions as concrete spiritual experiences, his immediate response was, "I'm afraid of voices and visions."

That's understandable of a young writer, just beginning to involve himself in the consistent writing process, just scratching the surface of going deep and taking chances. Of course, to the young writer, it doesn't feel like scratching the surface. The experience is the deepest, most profound he has felt thus far in his young life. It seems to lead to immediate insecurity, and fear of showing his work to anyone: release of those innermost thoughts, feelings, observations and determinations—laying bare the soul. Our senses and psyches have gone on point, commenced and completed the dance or hunt, and have captured a draft of a poem or story which we dare not show to anyone except the one or handful of humans we intimately trust. We feel as though misunderstanding or rejection's only result must be death. That's the feeling.

Eventually we show it to someone. We receive either acceptance, approval, praise, or responses of confusion, rejection, or even ridicule. The responses will determine how we temporarily move forward, or not. Praise can guide us back to the writing desk. Ridicule can lead us to put the draft away, or maybe even burn it.

This can prove true even deep into the writing. Look at these two paragraphs from "The Big Read" on the website of the National Endowment for the Arts:

Any claims for To Kill a Mockingbird *as a book that changed history could not have seemed more far-fetched one winter night in 1958, as Nelle Harper Lee huddled in her outer-borough New York apartment trying to finesse her unruly, episodic manuscript into some semblance of a cohesive novel. All but drowning in multiple drafts of the same material, Lee suddenly threw open a window and scattered five years of work onto the dirty snow below.*

Did Lee really intend to destroy To Kill a Mockingbird*? We'll never know. Fortunately, in the next moment, she called her editor. J.B. Lippincott's formidable Tay Hohoff promptly sent her outside to gather all the pages back—thus rescuing* To Kill a Mockingbird *from the slush.*

Lee's ego-centered fear gave in to temporary despair. But after heaving out the manuscript, obviously that inner voice urged her immediately to seek help, and from the right person. Then that person's determined voice guided her to recover her work and continue the creative process.

Reading the NEA story of Lee's struggle led me to poetry, imagining her experience:

BURNING IN SNOW

Harper Lee, flaming inside with despair,
shoves open borough apartment window,
hurls five years of scarred pages through ice-air
night, watching them flutter and flip through snow,
fall to rest in frosted holly bushes
and over frozen lawn. She calls Tay, who
yelps, *My god! Go get them! Now!* She rushes
down, creaks through New York crust, ignoring flu,
burning in snow, cursing her cowardice.
Gathering those raw leaves, she starts to cry,
struggles to hear drunken Truman's advice
about loneliness; mutters to dark, *Why
do we even try?* Feels readers hate her.
Doesn't know the Pulitzer awaits her.

Roger Armbrust
July 11, 2013

In the end, I believe, it's the inner psychic impulse, the spirit or Muse recognizing our gift more than we do, that will determine our path.

The poet and teacher Miller Williams, during a poetry workshop back in the 1970s, put this challenge to the attendees:

"You've got to have the drive," Williams told them. "If you have the drive and not the talent, you will be frustrated. If you have the talent and not the drive, you will be ashamed. If you have the talent *and* the drive, you will find out life is hell."

I was covering Williams' workshop for a local newspaper those years ago. When I wrote about his opinion, I followed his quote with this response: But you may also find the joy of creativity.

There's a lot I didn't know about William James or concrete spiritual experiences or the creative process back then. I didn't use brief invitations like "Go Deep. Take Chances." But I obviously had within me a sense of the faith and action James speaks of. While I was covering the workshop as a journalist, I also had been writing poetry, and—at a later workshop—I even read some of my poems.

I listened to Williams' statements, and internally responded with my own understanding: "…you will be frustrated." Yes, I can see that. "…you will be ashamed." Yes, that makes sense. "…you will find out life is hell." Wait. No. Life can be hell, yes. But it doesn't have to be.

I had experienced that drive, and still do. I had felt both frustration and shame, and hell. But I also had experienced deep joy with the writing process.

Jerry Whitley, a dear, creative friend in New York, a writer, singer, and songwriter now living in Vermont, once offered what he understood to be an Ernest Hemingway quote: "It is good to have written." Even then I said, no, not for me. I understand that statement, how writing can be challenging, draining, even fearful and perhaps terrifying as we plunge deep. I had experienced that in the early days. Not much now, decades into it.

But even in those early days I also looked forward to moving from work and people and becoming alone but not lonely, releasing in words, rhythms and imagery what swelled inside. And if it was loneliness that sometimes swelled inside, releasing that, too.

Looking back on all this, it seems to me that the difference in whether a writer's life is hell or joy gets back to faith and action, and especially faith. Not faith in a religion created by others, but in that spirit poets for centuries have called the Muse, the voice and rhythms of the Universe.

I think I felt that even as a boy, first picking up a pencil and starting to scratch out lines I considered poetry. As a teenager, I wrote more, but afraid to show it to anyone. And even as a young man, writing daily as a newspaper reporter. But even then, I didn't know what to call that drive, and hadn't examined poetry's history or where that drive might come from. Still, I felt it and seemed to trust it.

If you've read this far, you probably know what I'm talking about.

Gradually, if you stick with it, you begin to recognize the voices and visions that come to you. You begin to expect them, and welcome them.

I welcomed them in 2008 in this sonnet. My friend and mentor William Packard had died in 2002. I was listening to a song written and sung by Sandy Denny. I began to connect dots somehow: her song, images of her, and then of Bill and his small poetry book *Voices/ I Hear/ Voices* and its poems, each only three lines. Then the urge to write came:

VISIONS, I SEE VISIONS

Sandy Denny, dressed as in tintype, steps
off the album cover and kisses me.
I reach out, softly touch her stretched triceps,
our bodies glowing, pastel comets free
and flowing through Trifid Nebula, dawn
mountains of opaque dust coating us, pale
as angels. Now night here in Washington
Square Park, William Packard leaning on rail
next to me. We watch walkers pass. Poems
brief as breath slip through his lips, their spirits
singing. He grasps the small book, potent rim
of his hand raising it toward the moon, its
pages burning like stars. *Art never ends*,
he whispers. I watch his great form ascend.

The key, I believe, is that, if you stick with it, the Muse provides the gift of faith, which gradually replaces the fear that my young friend—who has yet to trust those voices and visions—spoke of.

But in this age, fear is very understandable. We grow up surrounded by entertainment media creating images of spirits and demons and space creatures meant to scare us, even haunt us after we've stopped viewing the movie or TV show. That constant contact from youth on can surely make one wary of the appearance of a voice or vision.

It is, of course, a common fear of humans. Just read or watch the classic, "A Christmas Carol," and experience with Scrooge his trauma when, first, the distorted, suffering ghost of Marley appears, and then the powerful spirits of Christmas confront him. But also focus on this: After Ebenezer gets over the initial shock of each appearance—

realizes the spirit's not there to harm or kill him, but help him—he actually eases from fear to some form of faith. He doesn't want to believe Marley but is afraid not to. Perhaps without even knowing it, he trusts each spirit because he realizes each is being HONEST with him.

I wrote in the introductory e-mail about the importance of honesty. And we'll talk more about that as we go. Its value in every human relationship is immense, and that's true of honesty with the writer and reader.

I also believe that honesty comes through examples of concrete spiritual experiences involving voices and visions. James covers examples of those in the lectures of his *Varieties* book, and I believe they're apropos for writers.

In one lecture, he quotes Walt Whitman's writing, sharing a voice and vision not his own:

I believe in you, my Soul...
...Swiftly arose and spread around me the peace and knowledge that pass all the argument of the earth,
And I know that the hand of God is the promise of my own,
And I know that the spirit of God is the brother of my own,
And that all the men ever born are also my brothers and the women my sisters and lovers,
And that a kelson of the creation is love.

The spiritual experience of creative writing is more than surface optimism, and even more than joy I cited in responding years ago to Miller Williams. I believe now it is the closest we can come in this life to complete communion with the divine. We experience it, learn from it, grow from it, and want to return to it as we do to an honest, passionate lover, with that same lovemaking intensity where we feel our 100 trillion cells meld, not only with another loving human, but with the Universe we share. Including the exhaustive satisfaction and peace that follows.

Yet, for us humans, that is always temporary, causing us to recall it, both its pleasure and pain. And, though perhaps our recognition of our limits causes us wariness, we still long to share again that concrete creative experience, and hope to return again to its challenge and fulfillment.

KEEP SOFT INSIDE

Keep soft inside your ever-sacred you.
Consider your 100 trillion cells,
each its own identity, each small room's
shrine of nucleus and DNA. Tell
yourself bedtime stories of each cell's life
as each of your lives, how each universe
connects the universe of you. Decides
what music moves you, which great poet's verse
melds you to its rhythms, its imagery.
Guides you to intimate friends, and perhaps
a mate. Leads each sense to long for the sea.
Cautions you to avoid fear's hidden traps.
Feel your tongue tip's touch as you whisper "love",
fitting the palate like finger in glove.

Roger Armbrust
March 8, 2015

responses to prayer

What is prayer?

If you want a one-word definition, you need only look at a scene from the film "The Misfits," written by the great American playwright Arthur Miller.

The characters—a couple of cowboy wranglers, their pilot buddy, and two women companions—have been out for a night of drinking. They raucously return to the farmhouse. The great cast of character actors—Clark Gable, Montgomery Clift, Thelma Ritter, Ely Wallach—stumble up the steps and inside. Only the beautiful Marilyn Monroe stops, watches them go in, then walks to the edge of the dark porch, gazes with lonely, lost eyes up to the night sky. She breathes quietly for a moment. Then she whispers one word:

"Help."

It's a brief but powerful expression; one that can control an audience who, in its silence, experiences the character's feeling of being lost, and the need to seek guidance, or even rescue, from some greater source.

Miller's single word also expresses a universe of meaning. It tells us the character believes that this higher source knows more than she does, sees more, has been observing her life and those about her, so understands explicitly what she needs, even more than she herself does. No need to explain details. Only surrender to the great, caring force and be willing to accept guidance.

Wallace Stevens' poem "Sunday Morning" includes a stanza imagining an early civilization expressing its surrender to its own god or gods, even seeing that power among them:

Supple and turbulent, a ring of men
Shall chant in orgy on a summer morn
Their boisterous devotion to the sun,
Not as a god, but as a god might be,
Naked among them, like a savage source.

William Packard found Stevens' entire stanza so meaningful, he injected it early into his book on the art of writing poetry. And no wonder. It's our genetic connection to the human wonderment of whatever great power is out there, and how we imagine it.

Stevens' chanters may or may not have expected a loving response to their efforts. But my experience, and those of other poets and writers and artists I hold dear, includes some form of trust that, if we show faith in the Muse, that great source will respond with guidance, through both the struggled wading and the seeming effortless flow.

We've spoken of Homer and Ovid and Akhmatova using prayer. Why? For the obvious reason that they believe they'll receive a loving response. And that belief, in turn, results in action, taking them through the writing process. Homer's *Iliad* and *Odyssey*, Virgil's *Aeneid*, Akhmatova's volumes of simple yet powerful poetry have risen from their honest conversations with a creative power they have come to trust. So, in their cases, the responses to prayer have been a sharing of classic creativity.

Now, anyone who's taken part in this process also understands this reality: Every day's a new day. And some days the loving Muse may respond with a caring "Not today." And the reality is we may not understand why. I've no doubt that had to have happened to the ancient poets and to Akhmatova, and most poets and writers down the line. The key for us is this: to trust the continuum of the process. That itself, I believe, is a faith the Muse infuses in us.

And to trust the process means to keep at it. I recall years ago reading an article in "Writer's Digest" by a professional writer who said he goes and sits at his desk every day, because that's his job. Some days, he noted, are better than others. Some days the words flow, some days they begrudgingly trod forth, and on rare days the Muse seems to ignore him. But his job is to be present so, when the Muse is ready, he's ready.

The word we writers commonly use for this is *discipline*. And that's right. But discipline, to me, seems to have gotten a bad rap. It seems to be handcuffed with an image of suffering, like what Miller Williams related with writing being a life of hell.

I think some of that comes from our experience as youth in school. If ever you acted out, you'd be sent to the principal's office to be "disciplined." And then we're constantly subjected in books, TV and films to stories about the military, and that rugged discipline designed for deadly force and survival.

But the writer's discipline, I believe, is not hell. I believe it's a gift from communicating with the spiritual source who wants us to write honestly and well: a result of the infusion of faith and impetus to action which leads us to begin placing one word after the other, one phrase after the other, until a unique whole exists. A unique whole which we realize we don't produce alone.

So, we approach prayer expecting a loving and guiding response, even if sometimes the answer is no, because we trust the main creator and the process.

And we, in turn, have our own response to the response, by

showing up and taking part in the process. And, in reality, that action of quietly showing up itself is a prayer.

SURGERY

My friend Kevin has written a novel.
Reading it, I slit open my fat gut,
peel out intestine, refuse to grovel
at truth of who he is, who I am; put
scalpel to peritoneum, descend
past serosa and muscle to lumen
revealing how I survive: first pretend
care for others while I fear rejection,
then, exhausted, surrender to spirit
and honest actions. They lead to healing
when I suture my past—once desperate
lies—through prayer and amends: change revealing
what I've always wanted but didn't know.
I finish a chapter. Renew my vow.

Roger Armbrust
March 20, 2013

changes of heart

As through prayer we feel fear lifted and replaced with infusions of faith and action, we also begin to experience changes of heart as we write.

Poetry, music and song through the ages, more than any other source, have expressed humans' deep desire for love, its futility and fulfillment. Humans expanded these arts further through staged drama and printed books, and then film, with all these arts distributed globally, and then available to massive audiences instantly through television and now the Internet.

We've spoken about fear of rejection, the incessant longing to understand and be understood, to hold and be held, to share the passion of love at every level: physical, psychic, spiritual.

Shakespeare, I believe, summarizes changes of heart in three brief statements: "Love all. Trust a few. Harm none."

I believe this is where the Muse leads our hearts in our writing, with one alteration: When dealing with the Muse, instead of "Trust a few," we can Trust All.

That doesn't mean we trust that every phrase we write is sacrosanct. It means we understand the balance between our human limitations in expression and the Muse overseeing the process. Memory and emotion can sometimes make us stumble as we go deep; we think we're using the right word, or have captured the perfect image, in our first draft. Then, as we go back over the writing and edit it, we connect more dots, better comprehend the overview, listen and may hear a better word or phrase, or discover a more appropriate, even more powerful image.

I'm recalling here the film "Finding Forrester," and Forrester sitting and typing with his new student, telling him, "We write the first draft with our hearts, and the second with our heads."

The honesty of that process leads us through our changes of heart, where we better understand the poem's persona or the story's protagonist, and we even trust what we don't understand because it may simply "feel right."

This "feeling right" leads me to a brief reflection on how the Muse will move a persona or characters to take over a poem or story, how the writer will be wise to let them take over, and see where it goes. We hear writers speak of this often, with characters developing minds of their own, and being propelled into actions the writer didn't expect.

I recall writing screenplays where characters appeared "out of the blue". I had no earlier thought about their existence, until suddenly they entered to help move the plot forward, and in their best instances to also more fully define the main characters.

Here's an example:

In my screenplay called "Hidden People" the 12-year-old boy Jody is caught up in a family drama that has overwhelmed him. He runs from his new home—in a strange town where he knows no one but his mother—down a Florida beach. I felt he needed a friend. But who? I had no one in mind at that moment in writing. But I had learned to trust the Muse, the process. Here's what happens:

THE BEACH. DAY.
JODY is running as hard as he can, tears in his eyes now. The boat and couple in the distance move gradually out of sight. He comes to a clump of palm trees. He is out of steam, and stumbles to the trees, where he plops to a seating position, pulls his legs in, putting his head between his knees, and he sobs. Gradually his crying lessens. He breathes deeply, and raises his head.

> JODY
> (surprise and fear)
>
> Oh!

Right in front of his face, in ECU (extreme close up), is the face of MAGGIE COBURN, also about 12 years old. The face and eyes are beautiful, but her head is shaved, and she has rings in her nose and both ears. She gazes intently at Jody, then speaks to him ever so softly.

> MAGGIE
> (softly)
>
> You're a warrior.

Jody, sniffing, quickly begins to wipe tears from his eyes.

> JODY
>
> Wh…what?

> MAGGIE
>
> You're a warrior. Like Genghis Kahn.

                              JODY
        War…warriors don't cry.

                             MAGGIE
        Oh, yes, warriors cry. It opens their senses.
        They're more aware. It saves them in battle.

Jody watches her quizzically as she studies him.

                        MAGGIE (cont.)
        Come on.

She rises and begins to walk down the beach. We see that she wears an
old sweatshirt, cutoff blue jeans and sneakers. Jody sits and watches.
Maggie turns to him.

                        MAGGIE (cont.)
        Come on, Genghis.

Jody rises and catches up with her. She's walking with positive
aggression, and Jody attempts to fall in step.

                              JODY
        What's your name?

                             MAGGIE
        Maggie.

                              JODY
        Mine's Jody.

MAGGIE

To them you're Jody. To me, you're Genghis.
They name us what they want, and
then we name ourselves what we want.

JODY

So, is Maggie their name or your name?

MAGGIE

It's *my* name. They call me Vi.
It's short for Violet. Is that dumb or what?
They met in college at New York University
and fell in love.
He gave her violets, because that's the school's
flower. So because they want some pukey
memory, they gave me a pukey name.
But I am now Maggie.

JODY

How'd you pick Maggie?

MAGGIE

It's for Margaret Sanger. She worked for birth
control to save women's lives. She was a
warrior too.

JODY
(impressed but softly)

Wow!

MAGGIE

Here we are.

They've arrived at a large cluster of palms. Maggie goes inside, and Jody follows. There in the middle sits a small, clear pond. They gaze quietly at it.

MAGGIE (cont.)
Genghis, welcome to The Mystic. I named it that.
There are spirits here.

She sits and crosses her legs yoga-style. Jody's in awe at the silence, and the soft sunlight slanting through the leaves into the water. He sits and watches her as she gazes into the pond. Then he, too, turns and focuses, both in a nature meditation.

(END SCENE)

I confess: I fell in love with Maggie. She's no one person I've known, but a compilation of personalities in my experience and imagination. That's what writers do: We'll mix and blend to come up with a character who helps the poem or story or script. And Maggie proved important: a catalyst to encourage Jody to grow as the story moves forward.

I've had the same experience often in poetry writing, where a character or image may enter, or a scene entirely change, simply because they should. When the Muse, the inner voice, takes you there, it's important to trust the process.

To me, that's a part of the joy of writing, of sharing with the Muse creativity's endless possibilities. And when you do that, you feel your heart change and your love for life, your sense of total involvement in existence, grow.

FINGERTIPS

By day I reach out and touch fingertips
of trees and plants, thank them for vital air.
By night I reach up and touch fingertips
of stars, praise their silent songs. I compare
them to candlelight, their sacred vespers
of spirit. Always within day and night
I touch your fingertips, utter whispers
of thanks for you. If I find you in sight
or not, I do this. Your fingertips pressed
soft to mine seem to define existence,
express through our universe all that's blessed.
Our fingertips preparing food, presence
of life's continuum, feel earth's command
to love all through flexing our gentle hands.

Roger Armbrust
August 3, 2014

infusions of faith/deliverances from fear

Our writing consciousness dwells in its true joy, I believe, when it melds our experience, imagination, and dreams, as Rilke encouraged. And we reach and abide in that blessed place when we open to the Muse who delivers us from the fear of going deep, and infuses us with the faith to take chances.

When and how does the Muse infuse this faith? In a universe of ways.

Robert Frost late in life shared this experience in an interview with John Sherrill. He remembered when he was a boy in New England:

"I had gone to Cambridge one day," Frost recalls, "and I was standing in a bookstore, thumbing through Francis Thompson's famous religious poem, 'The Hound of Heaven'. I became fascinated with his idea that we are not seeking God, but God is seeking us. I bought the book. I spent my carfare for it, and I had to walk home."

Frost, in his Frostian way, understated Thompson's poem. Thompson's celestial hound doesn't just seek the poem's persona, it relentlessly pursues the fearful, fleeing human and, at last, apprehends and consumes him with love.

Frost spoke, too, in the Sherrill interview of gaining confidence (which we might also consider a deliverance from fear):

"Where is it that confidence and faith separate?" he asked. "…We have confidence in the atom. We can test the atom and prove that it is there. I have seen an old New England farmer try to test God in this same way. He stood in his field during a thunderstorm and held his pitchfork to heaven and dared God to strike him. You just can't prove God that way."

What I hear Frost saying: You can't go get God, the Muse. You have to prove the Muse by awaiting her, as Akhmatova wrote. And sometimes, as Thompson wrote, you may flee her in fear until you finally surrender to her endless pursuit.

Frost's personas seemed to prove God by viewing nature and the universe, from looking closely at a flower and connecting with human relationship, as in "The Telephone"; and by gazing at the stars through a telescope and reflecting on existence, as in "The Star Splitter":

Bradford and I had out the telescope.
We spread our two legs as we spread its three,
Pointed our thoughts the way we pointed it,
And standing at our leisure till the day broke,
Said some of the best things we ever said.

Rilke goes deep, speaking of faith and its effect on life in much of his writing, including *Duino Elegies*—his mystical poems infused with religious intensity—and his earlier *The Book of Hours*, through which he seeks God and examines prayer:

I rouse you with loud knocking, I do so
only because I seldom hear you breathe
and know: you are alone.
And should you need a drink, no one is there
to reach it to you, groping in the dark.
Always I hearken. Give but a small sign.

Later, when an established name, Rilke shows in *Letters to a Young Poet* how he's grown more confident of his aloneness, its rapture of feelings and insight and change, and the faith that abides:

Therefore, dear Sir, love your solitude and try to sing out with the pain it causes you. For those who are near you are far away... and don't expect any understanding; but believe in a love that is being stored up for you like an inheritance, and have faith that in this love there is a strength and a blessing so large that you can travel as far as you wish without having to step outside it.

So, we're back to love, and how through creative writing we express love in all its forms through connecting with all that exists, from fear and pain to ecstasy to our life-death continuum. And it seems that a faith in the process can consistently guide us through all of creativity's darkened, dim and well-lighted to brilliantly blinding corridors.

I WRITE YOU THIS

I write you this because we understand
each other. I write you this because we
both sense our eternal thread, precious strands
plaited and stretched to connect all. I see
this clearer than you, only because I've
been blessed with time to kneel closer, define
each fiber and how it entwines our lives.
You see it too, from your distance, fine lines
separating our vision, space measured
by depth of our fear to surrender, gift
of faith following our fall. I've treasured
you from first sight. Just why would spirit lift
us here, grace me with your presence, your plight
and mine in plain view? Look there. See the light.

Roger Armbrust
March 7, 2014

FAITH BREATH

Breathe in great spirit's faith. Breathe out all fear.
So we begin each morning, meditate
immersed in deep rhythm, voices we hear
within our lungs and heart's voice pacing fate
through our body-mind-imagination's
thoroughfares to universe's endless
Yes. What is laughter but our soul's ration
of understanding All? Our eyes profess
symbols: sky and earth encircling night's vast
search for light. What are smiles if not brief hints
of truths we've learned matching senses' near past
with memory's vault? What do swimmers glint
from your undersea kiss if not love consumed
in Mother Earth's flowing symbol of the womb.

Roger Armbrust
March 1, 2012

assurances of support

In order to write—to go deep, to take chances—we must sit alone, and yet are never alone. Our trust often comes—at least I see, looking back, mine did and does—from the Muse's assurances of support, both directly and through the loving spirit of others. They may know they're offering it, or they may not, but it's that honesty and love within and of other humans which help support us through our vital periods of survival and advancement, including the holistic writing process.

My first support came from my family, who did it more through expressing their own faith and action than through deciding to simply help me. My mother Frances White Armbrust worked at nights and on weekends in local movie theaters in Little Rock, primarily The Prospect, and later another called The Heights, both long-gone now. She started work there when I was five years old and stopped when I was in the fifth grade.

I could walk alone to The Prospect, only about five blocks away from our home on Kavanaugh Boulevard across from Mt. St. Mary's Academy. And, as Mom worked, I could stay and watch movies as long as I wanted. And I did, to the point where I would memorize the characters' lines and from time to time, to the consternation of those around me, sometimes recite them out loud until the usher would arrive to threaten me with a quick escort to my mother's frowning countenance. That would always quiet me.

But Mom loved sitting at home with me, hearing my detailed accounts of the movies that really excited me. I didn't realize at the time I was being indoctrinated with the blessing of dramatic and comedic language written by some of the world's best, ranging from Shakespeare to American playwrights like O'Neill, Hellman and Saroyan to novelists like Faulkner, Fitzgerald, Hemingway and Steinbeck.

The Prospect even brought in a variety of British and other foreign movies, and I sat amazed particularly at films with Alec Guinness, such as *The Man in the White Suit* and *The Lavender Hill Mob*. I once gazed enthralled with a foreign-language film, Jean Cocteau's *The Eagle with Two Heads*. I was six or seven when I saw it, had no idea who Cocteau was, and doubt I followed the English text translation very well. I seem to remember the actors who played the queen and the young poet-assassin as capturing me with their magnetism. But I had mainly been intrigued by the film's title, and sat fairly patiently throughout, waiting to see that eagle with two heads. You can imagine my disappointment when the eagle never showed. But I still remember the startled realization that no such bird existed or would appear. And I still can see the film's end: the intense faces of the queen and poet-assassin facing each other lovingly, with one of them saying that, though they must part, "…we will be the eagle with two heads." I seemed to get that even at my young age, and still do: how two humans' experience together can bond them.

And then there was the constant flow of Hollywood musicals, which brought the endearing talents of Astaire and Rogers, Gene Kelly, Donald O'Connor, Debbie Reynolds, Jane Powell, Doris Day, Gordon McRae, and many, many more front and center. Those amazing lyrics burst forth with that grand music.

That near-daily practice of attending The Prospect and

experiencing its films in my young life, under my mother's watchful eye, obviously provided a powerful assurance of support and push toward becoming a poet and writer.

That was supplemented by support from my other family members. I recall my father Wilbur Wright Armbrust enjoying reading western and mystery novels, primarily Mickey Spillane (which leads me back to The Prospect where Spillane's films joined with film noir classics like *The Maltese Falcon* and *Double Indemnity*, all impressing the young viewer's psyche).

My sister Joan—eight years older than I—began taking dancing lessons at Dorothy Donaldson's studio at a young age through her teen years. Joan carried that introduction into little theater work at Little Rock Junior College. She followed that for over a year to New York where she studied dancing and acting and experienced the deeply humbling cattle calls. Then she moved to Memphis where she modeled at Goldsmith's while also dancing and acting in local theater until she stepped away and settled into a marriage.

My young self observed her through all that, attending her performances ranging from dance recitals, to LRJC's production of "Heaven Can Wait" (my first live play), her singing and dancing for social gatherings, and her dancing in a production of "The Cabalist of Dorrance" in Memphis. Then, of course, there were times she would pirouette and leap through our house at 3201 Kavanaugh, as dancers must. All this was drawing me closer and closer to the arts.

Then there was my brother Frank, my main keeper and my idol. Our father was a natural athlete who had grown up in Crossett, a lumber town in southern Arkansas. Dad had played basketball and baseball there, went on to play AAU basketball as a young man, then organized softball with Worthen Bank (where he worked as a teller and later branch manager) into his 40s. He also coached basketball teams at Our Lady of Holy Souls, including teams my brother played on.

Frank and I both had served as batboys for the Worthen softball team, experiencing the men's talents and camaraderie up close, including their beer-drinking sessions at Winkler's bar. following games across the street at Lamar Porter Field. Frank and I were naturally drawn to sports. Often, my older brother by five years (God bless him) was ordered to let me tag along with him when he went to play pickup games of basketball. This was particularly valuable to me during summers when Frank would go to War Memorial Pool, where high-school and college players would gather for pick-up games on the burning concrete court. I was in the seventh and eighth grade then, and would watch the older boys play, then I'd shoot around with them between games. If ever a time came when they only had seven guys, not enough for a four-on-four game, Frank would say, "Let my brother play." They were kind and patient enough to include me. I learned from them and moved forward to make all-state in high school and get a scholarship to play small-college basketball.

What's that got to do with writing, you ask? Everything.

My watching my father coach and brother play inspired me to play. And the more I played, the more my confidence grew in my physical ability, and my skill to think and react quickly as conditions on the court rapidly changed. This carried over to my confidence off the court, and the belief that, if I could learn from and improve as I performed with older players, I could probably succeed at anything I wanted. That is: to take chances and succeed.

THREE-MAN WEAVE

On basketball courts at Catholic High
and LRU, our practiced discipline
found graceful motion: two teammates and I
stretched the hardwood's width, so at ease within
our moves, timed with leather sphere passed from man
to man. We'd catch and toss with fingertips
(never the palms), flicking our cat-quick hands
as if swatting gnats, our shoes' rubber grips
yelping as they bit and released waxed floor,
passer cutting behind receiver, each
body barely missing each. I adored
the drill's court-length curves, our ultimate reach
to the goal. We swayed as an entity.
Our dance, I see now, formed infinity.

Roger Armbrust
June 23, 2007

This connection of films and sports led me to my best friend through my high-school years at Catholic High. Mike Moran and I had become friends when he joined us at Holy Souls in the third grade. I still recall us seeing *The Quiet Man* together at The Heights, then playacting our own fight scenes afterwards, recreating the cross-country fisticuffs of John Wayne and Victor McLaglen.

We went on to Catholic High together, playing B-team and varsity basketball, working on the school newspaper with Mike as editor and me as assistant editor, and we even broke lose and wrote satirical two-man skits we'd perform for Catholic Youth Organization events.

Our writing at Catholic High was primarily encouraged by Father (later Monsignor) George Tribou, who taught us junior and senior English. Probably the first to really recognize our writing ability, he assigned us to run the high-school paper, *The Cicerone*, our senior year.

All this provided experiences which later would join imagination and dreams and translate into writing, for both Mike and me. He would eventually major in English, then teach for 40 years at Catholic High. Now retired, he's a published novelist, several times.

In high school, I was quietly starting to write poetry, but not showing it to anyone. I did begin showing it by college.

My junior year at Little Rock University, I edited the college paper, *The Forum*, and won a first-place editorial award from the Arkansas Collegiate Press Association. It was an editorial headlined "My Brother's Keeper", about my brother Frank, now a doctor, being sent to Vietnam. I closed the editorial with a poem. A *Forum* staffer later told me he had shown the poem to some writing friends at Louisiana State University, who had praised it. Certainly, for me, brief but powerful assurances of support.

The next year I wrote a poem and submitted it to *Voices International*, a small literary publication located in Little Rock. To my delight, the editor accepted it, and even included a written note of encouragement with the acceptance. Another assurance of support.

Then brief assurances came from others: my sister would grow excited when I'd show her poems. My friend Lee Rogers would mention to me how much he enjoyed reading my work, and still does.

The assurances of support began to come regularly as I moved into newspaper work. There's nothing like the daily writing practice for honing your craft, and nothing demands it more than a daily newspaper. This began after I had moved to Fayetteville and the University of Arkansas's main campus. I started "stringing" daily for the *Arkansas Gazette*, writing news and features about the U of A Razorbacks, primarily their football and basketball programs. I did that for three years, and I was hooked on writing as a profession, under the tutelage of the sports editor Orville Henry, an obsessive producer of paragraph piles himself, and Jerry McConnell, the quiet, insightful assistant editor, a veteran of sportswriting.

I also became good friends with Russell Cody, a Razorback running back, and his wife Susan. She was majoring in English, encouraged me to show her my poetry, and pushed me to continue writing. Two of those '60s summers, I worked in gubernatorial political campaigns, where I met a kind and caring attorney named Bill Henslee, who took me under his wing, explaining to me the political ropes. He was so steadfast in encouraging my poetry, he had his legal secretary type up every bit of it, so I could have a single typed manuscript. I still have a copy of that today.

Back in Little Rock after three years—having left Fayetteville for good—I got into advertising copywriting for Leavitt, Ginnaven and Dietz (who later added Lankford to the marquee). Bob Ginnaven was a highly creative writer, actor, and voice-over artist. He was also an honest, caring mentor who was greatly encouraging, leading me through the methods of tight, image-filled, saleable ad copy. I also edited newsletters for one client, Reynolds Aluminum, which operated several Arkansas mines and plants. All this, as I continued learning to work with words, tight and in the right order.

Then I moved to hard news, serving as both a general assignment and then city hall reporter at the *Arkansas Democrat*, the state's largest evening newspaper. McConnell had moved there as managing editor, knew my work from the Gazette, and immediately hired me. Here is where I experienced the real maturing process: hard news, real life and death, functioning society, culture, politics and government. What I learned there from my fellow reporters, from Ralph Patrick the city editor and the entire newspaper process is immeasurable.

The daily writing carried over to my poetry. My wife Carolyn was encouraging me, and I began to publish locally. Alan Leveritt, an LRU student working part-time at the Democrat, had begun publishing a small, independent newsprint tabloid called *The Arkansas Times*. He would eventually build it into a small statewide publishing principality. Alan's wife Mara Leveritt, who worked with him on the *Times* (and now a noted nonfiction book author), really liked my poetry and began publishing it. Then Wade Rathke, who had started Arkansas Community Organizations for Reform Now (ACORN) in Little Rock, asked to publish a small selection, and did so with a nice center spread in the ACORN newspaper, *The Advocate*. I also briefly hosted a poetry radio program on the local educational radio station KLRE.

I then met a wonderful poet John Biguenet (now a respected

poet, novelist, playwright, and translator). Fresh off of a masters at the UofA, he was working in the Poets in Schools program. I interviewed him for a *Democrat* article. He and his talented artist wife Sha quickly became friends with Carolyn and me. John and I published a first edition of a literary magazine called *Black&White: A Review of the Arts*. Under John's leadership, we were able to garner work from some solid talent. I borrowed money to publish the first issue. Carol Gaddy with the Arkansas Arts Council offered strong support; but her commission decided to concentrate funds on established groups and new performance art that year. So there was no second issue of *Black&White*.

This was in the 1970s. And this is when I met Ted Parkhurst, one of my two greatest creative supporters. He had become a mainstay of the local literary scene, starting a small publishing company called August House, taking his books and marching door to door, making sales.

Ted encouraged me to gather a selection of poetry, saying he would publish it. I did and he did in 1979: the book *How to Survive*. In the early 2000s, when I had returned to Little Rock from New York, Ted and I would work together for three years, starting Parkhurst Brothers Publishers, with support from Cecelia and Drew Kelso, Ted as publisher and me as editor in chief. We produced twenty-three books before I stepped away to concentrate again on writing. But Ted's constant encouragement has led to his publishing three other books of my poetry, a first novel and an in-process second one, and to lovingly badger me into writing this book on creative philosophy.

I should also mention that I stepped away from this book for a while—still writing poetry and columns on economics and politics—but stuck on whether I could even continue the book. That is, until my loving daughter Catherine, home for Christmas from teaching art at the University of Missouri, asked me what had happened to the manuscript.

"I wrote a couple thousand words, and couldn't think of anything else to say," I told her.

"Well, you have more than that to say," she responded. "I'm already using some of your creative philosophy in my teaching. I think you should get back and finish the book."

I looked her in the eye and said, "Okay. I will."

And here we are.

(I also must add here in the present a loving *thank you* to my brother's wife, Kay Scribner Armbrust. I discovered recently that she has spent the last 12 years making hard copies of every poem, mostly sonnets, I've placed on my online blog "The Sonneteer," started in 2007—a magnanimous, dedicated process from her, since the blog contains over 1,000 poems.)

Meanwhile, back in '79 when Ted was publishing *How to Survive*, I—divorced and restless—decided to move to the Northeast. Long story short, I moved to the Jersey Shore, was involved in writing, editing, publishing, and teaching, receiving great encouragement from the poet/writer H.A. Maxson, writer/professor David Martin, professor Robert Rechnitz (who insisted that writers should "break glass"), the gifted local theater director/producer Paul Chalakani, along with professor Gwen Neser, who I moved north to live with, and the amazing Manhattan-based psychologist/philosopher she introduced me to, Dr. Harry Royson.

Then in 1990 I moved into Greenwich Village. I spent nearly 15 years there, where I met a legion of dedicated, creative people: the brilliant writer/editor/publisher Tom Tolnay; the insightful, relentless poet/novelist Charlie Smith; prodigious, precise novelist/

short story writer Rick Moody; and courageous, unflinching writer/ actor Kevin Patrick Dowling; the masterful slide guitarist David Tronzo; the lyrical, mystical composer/musician/singer Cynthia Hilts; the untiring, giving writer Sara Dulaney and veteran, endearing book editor Marcia Markland. All these wonderful souls proved major assurances of support for me with their own special, individual depths of honesty, sharing and skill. From listening to and reading and watching them I've learned much about the art of creativity and living.

I must also note the assurances of support from associating for a decade in New York with the talented staff at *Back Stage*, the national trade publication for professional performing artists. Editor Sherry Eaker had brought me in as their first news editor, then national news editor. They were more than journalists. Most were also artists in their own right, dedicated to the living theatre. For example, Michele LaRue, who edited our feature sections, is an actress who performs one-woman shows; senior editor Erik Haagensen is an accomplished playwright, lyricist and director. David Sheward, working as managing editor, developed into a noted theatre critic and has authored biographies. I watched national theater editor Leonard Jacobs enter as a theater critic and grow into a solid journalist; I eventually respected and trusted him enough to ask him to review my columns before publishing them because, as Tom Tolnay loves to say: "Everybody needs an editor." From 2012 to 2017 (when I broke away to write a novel), I worked closely with Leonard on the online arts/politics blog *The Clyde Fitch Report*, which he founded. Communicating with these special souls every day helped me expand further the craft of writing and editing.

But the support which helped me most realize myself as a poet and writer came from William Packard, who became my creative mentor. I remembered his brilliance, skill and loving care in a column first published on the news/culture blog *reality: a world of views*, which I co-founded with Drew Glover and Bill Asti. I give you that column here, and offer you all the memories in this chapter to express the importance of loving humans who form an assuring fortress of support with the Muse as we move forward to go deep, take chances.

(Published first on the website reality: a world of views)
Mentor: Remembering William Packard
by Roger Armbrust · January 5, 2015

In the early '90s, I was living in a fourth-floor walkup studio apartment on Sullivan Street in Greenwich Village, between Bleecker and Thompson streets. A block and a half from Washington Square Park, the area being swallowed up by New York University.

I was freelancing fulltime as a writer for Howard Sherman Public Relations, a one-man shop housed in a basement office of an apartment building at Broadway and Bleecker, an easy walk from my residential cell. Howard's clients were primarily in the post-production industry, providing support for commercial film and radio. I'd write press releases and features, and man the phone along with a part-time gopher, usually an NYU undergrad.

I had been writing poetry since high school, publishing a little though rarely sending anything out, and continued that when I moved from Little Rock to the Jersey Shore in 1979—the year Ted Parkhurst published my first book of poetry, *How to Survive*, for August House in Little Rock.

By 1990, nearly dried up creatively, I was concentrating on pounding out the PR.

But I had met a wonderful friend, Sara Dulaney, who lived and worked nearby—a marketing writer for NYU's division of continuing education, a behemoth consisting of hundreds of professionals teaching primarily evening courses in every field imaginable.

Sara knew I was looking to earn more money, and recommended me to the dean of continuing ed's writing section, who hired me to teach a professional writing course. While doing that, I learned that a continuing ed teacher could also take a free class. I looked in the vast catalog and caught sight of a poetry-writing course.

I soon happened to be talking long-distance with my friend Harry Maxson, a poet/writer who publishes under the name H.A. Maxson. We had met and become close while living on the Jersey Shore. Max had since married, and he and Maureen had moved from Jersey to Mississippi, where he completed his PhD in poetry at Mississippi State University. (Now they live in Delaware, where he continues to write.)

"I'm thinking of getting back into writing poetry," I told him. "I can take a free class at NYU, and I've found one."

"Who teaches it?" Max asked.

"A guy named William Packard."

"Shit!"

"What?"

"He's probably just the best poetry editor in America."

"Uh...maybe I shouldn't take it then..."

"No! Take it. It will be good for you."

Packard cut an imposing figure, both physically and professionally. Physically, he appeared bearlike: perhaps 6-2 or 6-3 in height, barrel-chested, weighing probably 250, a dark and grey-stained full head of hair and beard, thick eyeglasses, and a deep but whispery voice which immediately created intimacy while also indicating he knew something you didn't. A voice that a classroom of 25 could still hear, usually because we were struck silent by his resume.

A New Yorker, he had majored in philosophy at Stanford, hobnobbed with the Beats and other San Francisco poets. Returning to New York, he had published poetry, plays, novels and nonfiction. His awards ranged from a Frost fellowship to being honored at the White House.

As for his teaching poetry, his editing, and his impact on poets, hear how Wikipedia summarizes it:

Beginning in 1965, when he inherited from Louise Bogan the poetry writing classes at New York University's Washington Square Writing Center, Packard taught poetry and literature at NYU, Wagner, The New School, Cooper Union, The Bank Street Theatre, and Hofstra, as well as acting, and playwriting at the HB Studio in Manhattan. Among his books, he is the author of The Art of the Playwright, The Art of Screenwriting, The Poet's Dictionary, The Art of Poetry Writing, and The Poet's Craft: Interviews from the New York Quarterly.

Packard was editor of the New York Quarterly (NYQ) for 33 years—from its founding in 1969 until his death in 2002. He published 58 issues. Poet and novelist James Dickey called Packard 'one of the great editors of our time'. Cited by Rolling Stone as 'the most important poetry magazine in America,' the New York Quarterly earned a reputation for excellence by publishing poems, and for its 'exceptional in-depth interviews' with the prominent poets W. H. Auden, John Ashbery, Paul Blackburn, Richard Eberhart, Stanley Kunitz, Anne Sexton, Charles Bukowski, and W.S. Merwin, among many others. In fact, NYQ has, in its thirty-year career, published virtually every important poet in the nation. But the magazine is equally acclaimed for supporting the work of lesser-known poets. The poet Galway Kinnell once said of the magazine, 'The New York Quarterly serves an invaluable function—and that is finding and publishing wonderful talents—such as Franz Douskey, Antler, Pennant, Lifshin, Inez, Moriarty—who may not have the recognition that their work so richly deserves.'

Truth is, I didn't know all that when I walked in for the first time to face him. Otherwise, even Max's caring encouragement may not have carried me there. But once arrived, my relationship with him immediately began to root and grow.

NYU had evidently sent him a memo telling him another teacher would be taking his course. After that first class, he walked up to me.

"How's your course going?" he asked softly.

I don't remember what I said. Probably a muttered "fine." But we talked briefly, and his gentle welcome seemed to open the door for me.

Bill would provide handouts each class on a different poet, e.g. T.S. Eliot or Robert Lowell. But he would devote the entire class to the students' poetry. He'd have every student provide him a poem each week, then have copies of it for the entire class the following week. By then, he'd have marked each poem. But before he'd return it, he'd have each student read the poem to the class. The students would comment, and Bill would summarize, then give the student the poem with his written critique and suggestions.

I found the course so valuable, I took it twice. When the first course's final class had ended, I shyly walked up and handed him a wrapped gift. It was my first book, *How to Survive*. Earlier, I had found in the NYU library a copy of Bill's book of three-lined poems, *Voices/I hear/voices* (1972). Within it was a poem which read (and I hope I have this right, since I haven't seen it in years) "I bleed/when/I teach". Using that image, I had inscribed my book with this note to him: "Thank you for bleeding on me."

A couple of days later, a small packet came in the mail. It was from Bill: a note praising my book's poetry, and a reprint of his father's obituary, along with a sonnet sequence showing an unhappy relationship with his mother. So moved by this gift, I could only constantly pace my small studio like a caged lion, disabled really to do anything else.

Our classroom was in an NYU building bordering Washington Square Park. Occasionally, after class, we would walk through the park together, talking. Then he would head northwest to his apartment on West Fourteenth Street, and I would turn south to my studio. The experience eventually led to this sonnet a decade later, five years after his death at 69 on Nov. 3, 2002:

NIGHT OF THE HUNTER

William Packard, my creative mentor,
often lamented to his poetry
classes how Manhattan's night sky tortured
artists: grazing herds of stars fallen prey
to those two voracious wolves—smog and lights.
Through years of walking Greenwich Village streets
or Washington Square Park, we'd cherish nights
when Venus peeked through. Seldom we'd just greet
the moon. Once, through winter's bitter cold, I
limped lonely past NYU's library,
turned on LaGuardia, looked up and sighed,
"Oh, my. Hello." Orion's glow carried
clear and bright as lovers' eyes down to mine.
I felt caressed, warmed, lost in the divine.

July 16, 2007

A year later, listening to a Sandy Denny song, I began reflecting on it, on Bill's *Voices* book, and on talking with him in the park:

VISIONS/ I SEE/VISIONS

Sandy Denny, dressed as in tintype, steps
off the album cover and kisses me.
I reach out, softly touch her stretched triceps,
our bodies glowing, pastel comets free
and flowing through Trifid Nebula, dawn
mountains of opaque dust coating us, pale
as angels. Now night here in Washington
Square Park, William Packard leaning on rail
next to me. We watch walkers pass. Poems
brief as breath slip through his lips, their spirits
singing. He grasps the small book, potent rim
of his hand raising it toward the moon, its
pages burning like stars. *Art never ends,*
he whispers. I watch his great form ascend.

July 2, 2008

But while he was still living, and after he had come to trust my poetic judgment during that first poetry-writing course, he asked if I'd like to join him and a small group who would screen poetry for the *New York Quarterly*. I jumped at the offer.

We would meet regularly at Bill's apartment. He'd divide the still-sealed mail (NYQ yearly receives thousands of submissions) among the four or five of us. They included, among others, Erica Smith, who later became an editor at Random House; Stephanie Dickinson, poet, novelist and co-publisher/editor of the literary journal *Skidrow Penthouse*; and Raymond P. Hammond, who eventually lovingly looked after an ill Bill's affairs (he suffered a stroke in 1996) and took over as editor-in-chief of NYQ.

Filtering through each submission, usually of three to five poems, we'd choose a rare one for the selection stack. Bill would then take those and make the final decision about which poems to publish in NYQ. A couple of days after each session, the mail would bring a postcard, one side usually with an unpredictable image, the other with a note of thanks for screening from Bill, typed on his IBM Selectric which he refused to surrender to the computer age.

One of my most moving experiences in Bill's apartment occurred one day when he and I were alone, talking. I had stood up, preparing to leave. He remained seated in his writing chair, his leather-bound, legal-sized yellow writing pad in his lap, ink pen in hand.

He said to me, "You know, Roger, these college writing programs have it wrong. They preach to young people how they need to get published. But I don't believe writing is about getting published. I believe it's about the relationship between me and God."

As he said "me" he pounded once, hard, on his chest. With the word "God," he slapped his hand down solidly on his open writing pad.

I nodded and said, "Well, I agree, except to me it's this." I pointed straight up, then to my heart, then to his writing pad.

He gave a quick nod, and huffed, "Good!"

Being in Bill's apartment itself created a physical/psychic literary experience, which I eventually tried to relate in this poem, later published in NYQ:

BEETHOVEN'S BUST

for William Packard

You've moved Beethoven's bust
from your main room—
crowded with head of Zeus
statue of Venus holding apple
bust of Shakespeare
framed Patchen poem
model's color picture
and b&w of old professor
all above bookshelves
filled with leatherbound volumes
of modern and ancient classics
their browned pages
patched with bright red and yellow
smears of your highlight markers
flashing each ultimate phrase—
to your bathroom's toilet top
where seeing it on Sunday
I recalled stories of him
reclused in dungeon-dirt room
ignorant of stench
from week-filled waste pot
and lack of light from lone candle
alert only to spirit symphony and
ink pen scratching on parchment
great phrases no one else had ever heard

About halfway through taking Bill's course the second time, he came up after a class, saying that, in a couple of weeks he needed to go out of town. He'd have to miss one class. Would I teach it for him? Astounded, I agreed to.

I confess I prepared for that class diligently. Before he left, Bill and I met at a diner on Eighth Avenue for dinner and a talk. He provided me his handouts for the class.

"I've done some extra work on this," I told him. I knew his handouts would cover Robert Lowell. "I went to the NYU library and got a couple of tapes of Lowell reading. I'd like to play a couple of selections for the class."
He liked that idea.

"One of the tapes is of Lowell reading at the 92nd Street Y," I said. "I was wondering if maybe you heard him read there?"

"Roger, I introduced him."

Humbled, I smiled and said, "Bill, sometimes I forget where I am."

He had hosted those poetry readings at the 92nd Street Y.

He also had a poetry course at the New School of Social Research, and had to miss a class that same week. I covered that one for him also.

The following year, 1994, in the midst of a snowy winter, Bill had stepped out of a building onto an ice-slick sidewalk, slipping. His heavy frame plunged down directly on his leg, breaking it in three places. He called to inform me of this.

"I'm not going to be able to teach my poetry-writing class this spring," he told me by phone from the hospital. "Will you teach it for me?" I told him I'd be honored. And I meant it. Those brief fill-ins for his two poetry classes, along with my experience teaching my own class, helped greatly in preparing for taking over his NYU course that spring.

Also that spring, after a long day of writing and editing and an evening of teaching, I trudged back to the Greenwich Village studio, first checking the mailbox. I recorded in a poem what I found, and sent it to Bill:

LAST NOTE
Back from teaching class
where I was dull as gruel
and patterned as gray plaid
three envelopes plopped
from my mailbox:
Money Mailer
NYU
NY Quarterly
I saved two coupons
for cheap sedans
to Newark Airport
I tossed down
NYU paycheck
wrapped in green tile pattern
like a busroom floor
symbol of my worth
to their Revenue Div.
It plopped like
a mucous-stiff
handkerchief
on my mattress
I tore return
address end
printed NYQ
paper tan & smooth
White paper slipped out
photo fell in my lap
of Bill Packard seated
bedside at St. Vincent's

right leg pale
as a late-night nurse
reflecting fluorescent light
Left leg swelled
like thick neck
of a pissed drunk mick
skin stretched so tight
it could split from a flinch
with steel rod screwed
into bone
beneath the knee
rod latched to rod
circling the leg
like a pod
ready for launch into orbit
I unfolded white paper
to find loved copy
of Bill's last note from Bukowski:
eight lines of clean type
a three-letter signature
"Buk"
(its capital B like
a Roger Price droodle
of a whip resting on two breasts)
beside the trademark pen and ink
of tired old Santa's face
or a little boy walking in sleep

March 1994

By April 4, Bill had responded. He would always respond in writing, his IBM typing out his comments. As an example, here's his response to this poem:

good job – there are 3 characters in this poem:
first, you – with your feeling dull as gruel;
second, Packard – with his leg swelled like neck of pissed drunk mick
third, Bukowski – with tired old Santa's face, or little boy
walking in sleep. I sense there may be stronger relation
between 3 characters – teacher trying his damndest but still
feeling dull as gruel; another teacher who for all his damndest
gets leg out of whack; third, poet whose work is being taught,
tired old Santa, he has given all his Christmas goodies and now
is on his way out. All 3 characters are bereft, exhausted,
borderline beaten. Not to draw any generality about it, but
mull it over – am sure the 3 personas may be mask for one
persona, and title indicates LAST NOTE may be not just
Bukowski's but also Packard's and Armbrust's. Worth
working it over, see where it takes you –

Wm Packard [his eternal signature in ink]

Bill and the legendary poet Charles Bukowski had carried on a consistent, close correspondence, and Bill had published several of Bukowski's poems in NYQ.

Bill's mailing, which led to the poem, included a copy of Bukowski's note dated "2/24/94 4:28 PM". Bukowski would die on March 9, which led me to title the poem "Last Note". Here's what the note, double-spaced, said:

Hello Wm Packard:
Got your letter and photos from the hospital.
Sure the gods are testing you. You are a Leader and a Creator.
Remain in the fight. I can think of no other man as badly needed.
Stay. Endure.
I dispatch luck and love toward you.
sure,
Buk [ink signature and drawing]

The Readings

Bill also organized readings for the New York Quarterly, and invited those published in its pages to read. He held the readings at the New School. I read there a couple of times. To have a roomful, perhaps 50 New Yorkers who love poetry, applaud you after reading your own work is a gift. But there was no greater gift than, after my first reading, when I went to the back of the room and sat with Bill. He looked at me with tears in his eyes, and said, "That poem to your daughter was beautiful."

It was the title poem to my first book: *How to Survive*. This is the poem:

HOW TO SURVIVE

For Catherine, my daughter

Don't be afraid.
There is an order to all things.
In the blindness of the ocean floor
The spinefish survives.
The ancient snail finds its way.
Something that swims
Rises from the deep
Looks for and finds the land.
Through jungle trees
The lemur shrieks
Risks the leap
And discovers limits:
The indifferent suction of gravity.
It learns it can survive the fall.
In open space
The human walks and waits for stars
Studies how to survive.
I will tell you how:
When energy is gone
And your body can run no more
When pain has sucked you dry
When the spiders of
Fear
Sadness
Anger
Despair
Spit their poison through you
Stop.

Feel yourself.
Find the spiders
And let them go.
You will cry
Oh yes, and scream
And feel something in you
At last rip away.
In the peace that follows
In the silence of yourself
Think of the spinefish
Think of stars
Find a mirror or a pillow
And say outloud
What you know is true:
Don't be afraid.
There is an order to all things.

By 1996, I had taken a full-time job as the news editor for *Back Stage*, the NYC-based entertainment trade paper. I would eventually become the national news editor there. That full-time work, along with my night teaching, pulled me away from those weekend afternoons screening poetry for NYQ. I primarily stayed in touch with Bill with rare phone calls, and with poems I'd write for or about him, particularly for a birthday:

OLIVIER READS DAVID'S PSALMS

Birthday sonnet
for William Packard

I hear your clear voice these five years later:
"David's psalms are the greatest collection
of verses." As if on elevators,
we huddled in silence, blank reflections
on faces, left mute by your legend.
Stout-bodied, heavy-bearded, unoffended,
you with searchlight eyes refused to pretend
we had heard: "I'll repeat that." And you did.
Now, listening alone to Olivier's
sharp consonants crack like crisp lettuce,
I wonder how you'd respond to his ways
of altering tone from lisping softness
to shouts. Still, I pray for what David sees:
"…he shall give his angels charge over thee…"

September 2, 1999

Two years later that month, on Sept. 11, the World Trade Center tragedy occurred, just over a mile from my Sullivan Street studio apartment. The most meaningful way I felt I could respond was in a sonnet to Bill. I had begun writing sonnets consistently in 2000, I believe largely a result of reading his, and his teaching:

SEPTEMBER 11, 2001

for William Packard

The day before your sixth birthday, Auden
wrote of sitting in a dive observing
a city caught up in fear and awe. When
he did, I suppose someone was serving
you dinner miles away, Mamaroneck,
pre-party promises as you slurped ade
while Auden sipped ale, alone in the dark
bar's corner, napkin stained with words he made
stand at attention in eleven-line
stanzas. Some thirty years later, he told
you he had disowned those verses: a fine
line he had drawn for truth. Now, on this cold,
evil day, after you've turned sixty-eight,
we smell death, feel pain, can call his lines great.

A year and two months later, Bill had died of heart disease. Raymond told me he had found him lifeless that November day in 2002, seated in his writing chair, notepad and pen in his lap.

six basics of good writing

1. honesty

I keep two quotes about writing close to me:
The first from the poet Judson Jerome:

The poem is more important than the poet.

The second from D.H. Lawrence:

Whoever reads me will be in the thick of the scrimmage, and if he doesn't like it—if he wants a safe seat in the audience—let him read someone else.

It seems to me that honesty is the basis of every relationship, and if you're not honest, you don't really have a relationship.

This carries to the relationship between the poet and the poem's persona, the writer and the story's character, and the writer and the reader...and that first reader is you.

How do we define honesty?

The *Cambridge Dictionary* states:

Honesty: (of a person) truthful or able to be trusted; not likely to steal, cheat, or lie, or (of actions, speech, or appearance) showing these qualities.

I've come to believe the greatest opponent of honesty is fear, and the greatest ally is faith.

Fear seems to be a given in humans, a reaction which can aid our survival, but which can also freeze us and hold us back from growing and progressing. This is particularly true when it comes to revealing ourselves, first to ourselves, and then to others. And nothing is more revealing to ourselves and others than our rigorous, honest writing.

Revealing ourselves through honest creative writing takes a fearlessness, a faithfulness, and I believe that's not as much a personal decision as a gift of the Muse.

Society will push you toward fear of expression, and with that comes self-censorship, the murderer of creativity. Religions will try to censor you. Governments will try to censor you. Corporations, especially corporate media, will try to censor you. Fearful people will try to censor you. But your job is to remain fearless and faithful to the poem or story, to the persona or character, and let them honestly live through your expression. You must be, indeed, a courageous journalist, a relentless whistleblower, a clear, loving singer in the universe of creativity.

I'll share with you an experience which became a major turning point in my progression from fear to faith in creative writing:

Back in the '90s, I had just finished reading my poetry to a group at the New School in Greenwich Village, hosted by William Packard and the *New York Quarterly*. During the break, I looked up and saw a large man, perhaps 6'5" and 250 pounds, approaching me. He wasn't smiling, and my survival mechanism clicked in with the fearful thought, "Oh, hell, I hope I didn't read something that pissed him off!" Then the rapid reality (the Muse) shot in: "Armbrust, he wouldn't be at a *poetry* reading to get pissed off. He's here looking for inspiration, or perhaps just an answer."

When he reached me the big fellow stopped, dropped his eyes and began shuffling his feet. Then he said softly:

"I really liked that poem about your mother."

Surprise and warmth immediately rushed through me. He was looking at me now, and I replied just as softly: "Thanks, man. Thanks very much."

He didn't stay to talk, but immediately turned and walked away.

As I watched him leave, a greater reality suddenly occurred to me:

Rilke is right: If we *must* write, we use our experience, imagination, and dreams. And what's more, that's all we really have to go on. And that's all the reader or listener has to go on: his or her own experience, imagination, and dreams. And his experience, imagination, and dreams aren't mine; they're personal only to him. Yet, somehow, through our honest writing the writer and reader's experiences, imaginations, and dreams meld. Not perfectly. But strong enough to where our personal insights grow, and our lives become more meaningful, however slightly or greatly or briefly or permanently, through the process.

At that moment, I reached a new level of self-understanding: I no longer had to be afraid of what anyone else thought, or how anyone else reacted to my writing. Because I would never be able to perfectly mirror his or her experience, imagination, and dreams. I can only try to express my own experience, imagination, and dreams. Honestly and fearlessly, and therefore faithfully.

So that's what we work on today.

As I've grown more mature, and watched our society reach its present existence with a conniving government, military-industrial complex, and corporate media that wants us to fearfully see a terrorist at every turn in a mall or table in a coffee shop, I've become very frustrated with society's censorship and our self-censorship. I've expressed that through journalistic columns challenging government, military/industry, and media, and especially PBS when it censors visuals or language in dramas, especially during primetime when the kiddies are asleep.

And I even recently shot out a poem snapping both at Facebook and public television, and censorship's hypocrisy:

FACEBOOK DILEMMA

I can post photos of bullets and guns—
their mission to assault lif—day and night.
But I cannot display a man's penis
or woman's vagina—made to create life—
lest some "holey" adult be offended.
Same problem watching PBS prime time:
"Murder on the Home Front" offers close-ups
of a victim's severed tongue, yet blurs out
her bare breasts. Tits but not slashed tongue
might offend prudes and kids, I suppose
(a twisted policy for EDUCATIONAL TV,
one place you'd think would respect body parts).
Meanwhile, let's write s*#t and f@$k
but not shit and fuck, even though
everyone reading s*#t and f@$k
sees it as shit and fuck. I must admit
reading this might piss you off. Spare me.
All these words are in your dictionary.
Besides: I'm talking about honesty.

Roger Armbrust
December 4, 2015

The honest poet and writer must face life's reality with faith and fearlessness. And to do so might cost you dearly, might cost you your life—but not your spirit—as it did Lorca:

GARCIA LORCA

That stifling August afternoon, they dragged
him from the house. Granada homes huddled
in siesta, brief respite from day's rage
of civil war. Next day he'd feed puddles
of blood, his limp body slumped on Fuente
Grande's stark ground; then it would disappear.
Where the fascists buried him, none can say,
only suppose. Franco, slyly with fear,
would ban his poems and plays. Now his home,
Huerta de San Vicente, honors him—
white stucco museum where faithful come
to sense his spirit, recall his rhythms
of passion, phrases tight as leather gloves,
celebrate those drafts: *Sonnets of Dark Love.*

Roger Armbrust
April 4, 2016

But you can't let others' fears or force stop you. As you take on your own fear and others' fears in your efforts at honest creative writing, my experience is you'll need the gift of faith and assurances of support. And that is based on an honest relationship with the Muse.

Go for it.

2. general/specific

Our writing moves like an ocean wave from the general to the specific and back again, ebbing and flowing, carrying the reader forward.

I can make a general statement and then follow with more and more specific information:

General: I live on the planet Earth.
More specific: I live on the continent of North America.
Even more specific: I live in the United States.
Even more specific: I live in the State of New York.
And more specific: I live in New York City.
And even more specific: I live in the borough of Manhattan.
More specific: I live in Greenwich Village.
More specific: I live at 444 Thompson Street.
More specific: I live in apartment 222.

As I become more and more specific, I bring the reader closer to the persona's or character's personal experience.

You see film directors do this when they open with an "establishing shot" such as a view of Manhattan; then the camera will begin to dolly closer to a specific block, then closer to a building, then closer to a window of an apartment, then the camera moves through the window into the apartment's interior; then to the character slouching in a chair, holding a pistol; then closer and closer to an extreme close-up of the character's agonized face.

This is the way the film director moves from the general to the specific and more specific, carrying you into the scene and all its expectation.

Writers do this too, creating scenes in the reader's mind, moving from general to specific to bring you caressingly nearer.

Look at this scene from my novel *Pressing Freedom*, where the protagonist Reeves Franklin remembers his former lover in New York:

Heather had engulfed herself in literature and journalism at Brown, graduated with honors. Carried that to New York, where she had grown up in Brooklyn, then a clean-cut suburb in northern New Jersey. She worked as a self-help book editor with a small publisher, the Mason Press, in the Village. She had pushed the money-minded young owner to upscale the product. The ambitious editor tightly hugged and nurtured new young, intelligent writers who touted snappy styles and deep desires to be of service to others. And she quickly moved up to a senior editor position. Now she was splitting her time editing by day and caressing her own writing by night.

She was also caressing Franklin by night. And she had taken up the guitar. He loved watching her gentle hands sometimes struggling, sometimes dancing over the strings; hearing her soft soprano creating impromptu lyrics, which she would pause and write down when they felt right.

But they were also struggling with their secret demons, Franklin's known to him, Heather's repressed to the point she couldn't call up the source. Gradually she would.

This is how the writer brings the reader into the experience.

Note how the specifics inform you more about Heather's background and interests: Brown, New York (then even more specifically Brooklyn, then the Village), Mason Press (and her move from editor to senior editor), guitar, her soft soprano voice. Where could the writing have been more specific? What words or phrases would you use?

W.H. Auden is a master of the general statement, letting it and imagery carry the poem. Note his close to "Voltaire at Ferney":

Yet, like a sentinel, he could not sleep. The night was full of wrong,
Earthquakes and executions: soon he would be dead,
And still all over Europe stood the horrible nurses
Itching to boil their children. Only his verses
Perhaps could stop them: He must go on working: Overhead,
The uncomplaining stars composed their lucid song.

Auden gives us the name of Voltaire and his specific estate—Ferney—in the poem's title. But much within the poem involves generalities: an exile, a hospital, a joiner, trees. But he doesn't say specifically who the exile or joiner are, or the hospital's name, or the genus of trees. He offers some specific names like Pascal, Diderot and Rousseau who we may know through history, and Emilie and Pimpette, whom we must know through Voltaire's history to recognize. In the stanza above, he speaks of "wrongs" and "executions", but not the specific wrongs or killings. He's selective with adjectives: "horrible" nurses, "uncomplaining" stars. His active verbs are impactful: "Itching", "boil", "composed".

One thing about specifics in poetry: because poems are so tight, they don't give you much information. Either you know enough history about someone like Voltaire, or the specific may whet your appetite for more research and information. That's what happened to me with Auden's brief line:

Pimpette had loved him too, like scandal; he was glad.

I decided to research Pimpette, learned young Voltaire had tried to marry her, but the parents didn't go for it. That led me to concoct a sonnet of an imagined love letter from Voltaire to her:

MY PIMPETTE, MY LOVE

I close my eyes and see you still, strolling
the Herengracht's bank that first day we met.
Sun caressed your curls. Fishermen trolling
called out, praising your smile. I won't forget
how you blushed when I bowed, saluting you
as William's stadtholderette, your laughter
ringing like Zuiderkerk's bells. Your friend, who
frowned like a moistened prune, stalked off after
you kissed my cheek. Wandering Amsterdam,
we pledged love outside Rembrandthuis. Oh, how
you glowed in moonlight. I call you madame
still, despite my father nulling our vow,
your mother cursing my life. Now you're free
of me, but not my heart. ***François-Marie***

Roger Armbrust
December 27, 2007

In "regular" writing such as journalism, or memos or reports for business, the usual rule is we move from general to specific, and the specific data will support the general statement, making it clearer.

Creative writing is trickier, because the creative writer is dealing with the conscious, subconscious, and even unconscious, being guided by the Muse and story characters and poem's persona. It's that creative collaboration and intrigue that allow us to play with the language and take chances on when to simply be general or become more specific. It's the ocean wave not only ebbing and flowing, but curling into undertows, going deep.

I've come to know that providing specifics in creative writing may help the reader better experience a story or poem; but, even more powerfully, I believe it invites the reader to remember the past, far or recent, or imagine the future, and link the poem's or story's specific to something concrete in the reader's own experience.

In Thornton Wilder's classic play "Our Town" the two main characters Emily and George stop at Mr. Morgan's drug store for ice cream sodas. Watching that scene immediately took me back to growing up in Little Rock, sipping sodas as a young boy at Harrison's Drug Store on Kavanaugh. Doesn't that "Our Town" scene take you back home?

Once again, the poet or writer's use of specifics brings the reader deeper into the scene, and can invite writer and reader to connect with the human condition and the universe, as we saw with Auden's poem, closing with a view of the stars.

My old friend Lee Rogers and I, as very young men, met Auden briefly when he was in Arkansas. And so the British master poet has held a special place in my heart ever since. My creative mentor William Packard also spoke respectfully of interviewing him for *The New York Quarterly*, and that made Auden's impression even more indelible. As I moved toward finishing this book, I began thinking of Auden, and the other day wrote this sonnet, which hopes to catch you with specifics. Those specifics, if you know Auden, will be meaningful. If you don't know Auden, hopefully it will make you want to research and learn more about him and his relationships.

AUDEN

At his farm in Austria, nearing close
of this life, he reflects on their faces
and hands, their reactions each time he chose
his actions: Erika's fumbling laces,
hearing his offer to marry; Chester's
flex and flush—response to kissed fingertips;
Carson's smile at him playing the jester;
Benjamin's flinches to his manuscript
critiques. This week he'll train to Vienna,
perhaps visit Christ Church and the Schönbrunn,
read to the Austrian Society. When
that's done, he'll welcome sleep. His mind wanders
back to New York, his move there at start of war,
rejecting that poem he penned in the bar.

Roger Armbrust
May 20, 2016

3. imagery/concrete nouns/active verbs

Aristotle defined the power of imagery when he said, "The universal exists for, and shines through, the particular." The poet Miller Williams clarified that during a poetry reading by recalling a statement of his friend, the country singer/songwriter Tom T. Hall. Someone suggested to Hall that he write a song about ecology. He replied, "You can't really write a song about ecology. You need to write a song about an empty beer can." The more specific you are, the clearer the image and the more powerful the invitation to experience for the reader.

Imagery is the poet's and writer's most potent wand. It's the use of concrete nouns and active verbs to create solid pictures—images—on the reader's mind, producing an experience.

Here's my invitation to study an ice cube closely and see where it takes us:

ICE CUBE

Light flows so intensely through this frozen
crystal prism, faintest color's our result:
gray haze like London morning's explosion
of mist and smoke; then suddenly occult
transforming to translucence at center,
as clear as psyche following prayer.
Adjusting to this sculpture of winter,
the eye finds at its core a small layer
of droplets suspended like rain, or tears,
timeless reminder of what cleanses earth
and us. It chills the palm, predicts our years
to come: our living, dying, and rebirth.
Months from now, we'll consider how we felt,
passing it hand to hand, watching it melt.

Roger Armbrust
April 13, 2007

Look at the nouns and consider how they impress pictures on your mind: light, prism, color, haze, explosion, mist, smoke, translucence, center, psyche, prayer, sculpture, winter, eye, core, layer, droplets, rain, tears, earth, palm, years, months, hand.

Now look at the active verbs, i.e. verbs that describe action, and how they integrate to help create experience: flows, transforming, adjusting, cleanses, chills, predicts, living, dying, consider, passing, watching.

Active verbs put the nouns into motion, bring energy to the writing, and, at their best, effect a physical response from the reader.

When writing, prefer active verbs instead of "to be" verbs like "is" or "was", or dull verbs like "has" or "go". Ask yourself: Does my persona or character just "walk", or more actively "strut", "skip" or "stumble"?

Now, study this poem:

SUNRISE MANSION

The stench of urine floods this room
Grandmother
The stink flows from all rooms
soaks the halls
forever stains my nostrils
You no longer ask
why we leave you here alone
to let your brain dry like mucous crust
as if you never loved

I think often of your silence
of your voice once course as rust
leather lined
Now only rare whispers
Trickle through weak gurgles of spit
I blot your mouth with a cloth

Your head blends with whitewashed walls
Your eyes dull
grey as intestines
almost look at me
I tell you of my children's love
as skin clings to your cheekbones
wrinkles into stale dimples
telling me you hear

Oh I dissolve in the wetness of this place
the wetness of walls and floors
the wetness of beds, of eyes

the clotting wetness in mouths
nostrils, throats and lungs
in hard veins and bladders
blistered from excessive waste
The wetness
You

Roger Armbrust 1979

How does this poem affect you? Does it arouse your experience, imagination and dreams somehow?

Now, go back through it, list the nouns, the verbs with action. Consider how they create imagery that affects you. Then go through the poem again. Circle the phrases you consider the most powerful. Then jot a line, a paragraph, even a poem of how they relate to your personal experience.

Finally, go back through both poems, "Ice Cube" and "Sunrise Mansion" and look at the adjectives. Circle the ones you feel help the nouns create a clearer or stronger image.

Here's why I suggest this about adjectives: Poetry tends to be tight. William Packard loved to say, "Get in fast. Get out fast." In other words, don't waste words. Voltaire said, "The adjective is the enemy of the noun." If you have a strong concrete noun, that image may be enough. But not always. Sometimes the adjective can brush on that final stroke of color that makes the picture dynamic. You'll find that out through the editing process. The same goes for adverbs: use them only if they further empower the verb. Otherwise, leave them out to keep the writing tight.

CASUAL SEX

The adjective's
the enemy of the noun
Voltaire said
yet he used adjectives.
He must have meant
the dishonest adjective
assaulting the noun
like invading bacteria
making sweet milk go bad.
"I only have casual sex," she said.
"I understand perfectly," I said,
sliding out of bed
slipping on clothes.
"I once had a cat," I said.
"I never fed it
or let it out of the apartment.
But I played with it every day
and petted it every night
'til its bony little carcass
stopped breathing."

Roger Armbrust
February 2, 2001

4. metaphor/denotation/connotation

William Packard, in his book *The Art of Poetry Writing*, explains metaphor as well as anyone:

> *Metaphor and simile are extensions of simple image. Aristotle says in the <u>Poetics</u> that a good metaphor implies an intuitive perception of the similarity between dissimilar things, and he comments that it is the one gift that cannot be taught—one is either born with it or one isn't. Strictly, metaphor is a direct comparison; it is an equation or an equivalence, like saying A equals B—'A mighty fortress is our God,' or 'It is the east and Juliet is the sun.' Simile, on the other hand, is an indirect comparison using 'like' or 'as'.*

Look at the metaphors in this sonnet:

GERALD STERN

Jack just emailed a poem by Gerald
Stern, Pittsburgh boy, citing Galileo's
metaphor for the mind: paper scrap hurled
by wind. Anxious squirrel threatened by throes
of truck wheels, Stern says, best fits his writer's
psychic reality. I saw him read
once in the '80s—night of harsh winter
on the Jersey Shore—and began to heed
how poets prep us for the kill. Bald, plump,
grandfather's serene smile, he lured us toward
false security with baggy frame slumped
at the lectern. Then the hiding leopard
leapt from the dark, slashed minds with craft-sure claws
of piercing phrases, stroked hearts with his paws.

Roger Armbrust
August 7, 2007

See how Stern cites Galileo's metaphor, referring to his mind as a concrete object that creates a picture in your mind: "paper scrap hurled by wind". Then Stern calls his own mind an anxious squirrel threatened by wheels of passing trucks. And later I turn the bald, plump, serene-seeming grandfather into a hiding leopard who leaps from the dark.

You can also see here examples of how a metaphor's denotation and connotation bring greater depth to the poem.

The *Cambridge Dictionary* defines denotation as "the main meaning of a word, not including the feelings or ideas that people connect with the word." Connotation is "a feeling or idea that is suggested by a particular word although it need not be a part of the word's meaning, or something suggested by an object or situation."

Galileo's metaphor—a phrase rather than a word—denotes a piece of paper hurling in wind. But it connotes a psyche out of control, responding involuntarily to a barrage of thoughts and feelings. Stern connotes that his own mind feels under constant threat, leading to anxiety.

My metaphor for Stern denotes a hiding leopard, but it connotes a reason—either fearful or sinister—for his hiding. That's followed by the metaphor's action: leaping and slashing with claws, and yet also stroking hearts with closed paws. It still denotes a leopard, but it connotes that the beast both tears into its audience, bringing pain, while also caressing the listeners with care.

Do you see how metaphor empowers poetry's tight language by creating immediate pictures to impress the reader's or listener's senses and psyche, helping create an experience?

Now, take a look at the master Shakespeare and what's probably the most famous metaphor in literature. Examine how he extends the metaphor through the poem, using both comparison and contrast:

SONNET 18

Shall I compare thee to a summer's day?
Thou art more lovely and more temperate:
Rough winds do shake the darling buds of May,
And summer's lease hath all too short a date:
Sometime too hot the eye of heaven shines,
And often is his gold complexion dimm'd;
And every fair from fair sometime declines,
By chance, or nature's changing course, untrimm'd;
But thy eternal summer shall not fade
Nor lose possession of that fair thou ow'st;
Nor shall Death brag thou wander'st in his shade,
When in eternal lines to time thou grow'st;
So long as men can breathe or eyes can see,
So long lives this, and this gives life to thee.

Judson Jerome says that, to be a good poet, you must be aware of your world. Today, closely observe your world. Look for metaphors. Look for ways to energize them with active verbs. See if they lead you to a poem.

5. scrapping prepositions

I keep stressing how good writing involves "tight" writing, with no wasted words or phrases. In poetry, this rings particularly true, especially if you're limiting yourself to a specified number of syllables in each line, as I try to with a ten-syllable sonnet line.

One aid to this: paying attention to prepositional phrases. Does the phrase say exactly what I want it to say, or can I tighten that somehow? I've found that often a prepositional phrase can be replaced with an active verb by simply turning the phrase's noun into a verb. Examples: replace "he held her in reverence" with "he revered her"; or "he faced him in defiance" with "he defied him".

Shakespeare could have written "Shall I place thee in comparison to a summer's day?" But his poet's good sense obviously would have scrapped the dull verb "place" and replaced the prepositional phrase "in comparison" with the active verb "compare". That would give him the tighter, form-fitting ten-syllable line "Shall I compare thee to a summer's day?"

6. no absolute rules

I love to chat with folks about sports, particularly if a friend seems in a rut, unable to move forward. I recently had such a conversation with a stuck acquaintance, who is also a sports fan.

"You're a big Philadelphia fan, right?" I asked. "The Eagles. The Phillies."

"Yeah!"

"After they lose a game, what does the coach or manager usually say when interviewed?"

"We'll get 'em next time!"

"Well, he may say that. But what I often hear is his experienced solution, which seems to be this: 'We have to get back to basics. These are extremely talented athletes. And when we get back to doing the basics, then they're able to really implement and expand those talents, and we'll win.'"

My friend agreed with that assessment.

It's also true of writing. We can learn and apply basics of good writing, which we've discussed in this last section of the book. But those basics are meant to help us evolve and implement our own experience, imagination, and dreams to realize our personal vision, perhaps even create new forms of expression with our language.

William Packard wrote, and saw published, a novel with no punctuation—*Saturday Night at San Marcos*. He was going deep and taking chances, experimenting with a new writing style for himself. Look at this sonnet in which I played with the language, jumbling the normal flow of words:

I LONELY AM

I lonely am you of thinking night this
when smile shadowed of moon from above shines
and hill this beyond village lights small kiss
echo like memory like wind of pines
through falling long glistens shoulders your hair
over and breasts as angel's hand your flow
wing-like my face blessed on warm feeling air
eyes my one your eyes as light heart aglow
as beating one let oh night not this fade
body before your my body burn grass
in soft as one lie we smiles our bright made
stars of angels heaven's like flight in pass
over they us calling voices follow
to only they lovers place the allow.

Roger Armbrust
January 25, 2008

You've seen this going deep, taking chances throughout history, from the ancient Greeks to the Humanists to the Renaissance to the Romantics up to today. It is, in fact, your job to learn the basics, but to also stray from them. To "break glass" as Robert Rechnitz would encourage. To "make it new" as I once heard the poet James J. McAuley advise his audience.

In other words: there are rules, but no absolute rules. Dancing with the Muse leads to new steps. Robert Lowell, in conversation with James Dickey, referred to our poetry as a garden in our back yard. "We don't show it to everybody," he said. But we tend it and experiment, and revel in its development.

It seems in creative writing, experience tells us the basics don't come from man, but from the Muse. The ancient Greek Homer was blind, but prayed to the Muse and received words that led us to see gods, heroes, villains, and lovers. The Eighth Century historian Bede writes of the first English poet: Caedmon, an illiterate herdsman, blessed by the Muse through dream to begin to write songs. I summarized Caedmon's story, speaking to him, hoping to share his experience in this sonnet:

CAEDMON

The cattle curled in their protective sleep,
you lie on the pasture's rise, watching stars,
eyes slowly closing, staff by your side. Deep
dream brings a strange man to you. He implores,
Sing the beginning of created things.
You—who'd never read or written, who feared
(dull herdsman, I) at the abbey to sing
before those monks and St. Hilda—feel tears,
long to bolt. Yet you stay. Your tongue forms verse
you've never known, shocks you awake. Somehow
you recall all. Tell your foreman. His curse
muffled below his breath, he leads you, bows
to the abbess. She hears. Touches your face.
Turns her eyes toward heaven, praising God's grace.

Roger Armbrust
July 20, 2008

I have advised preferring active verbs to common, dull "to be" verbs like "is". But again, there are no absolute rules. Shakespeare uses the phrase "to be" to open one of his most famous Hamlet soliloquies:

To be or not to be…

But also notice how he follows "to be" with lines including the strong active verbs "suffer" and "opposing":

To be or not to be—that is the question:
Whether 'tis nobler in the mind to suffer
The slings and arrows of outrageous fortune,
Or to take arms against a sea of troubles,
And, by opposing, end them…

In your current day and age, you'll need to stick close to the Muse if you want to go deep, take chances, and stray from rules. I repeat: institutions will try to censor and limit you. And in this time of global dependence on technology, you'll need determination to keep and grow your own voice. In the '80s, those first days of developing computer graphics and animation, I interviewed the talented and highly respected computer animator Jim Blinn with Jet Propulsion Laboratories in California. In the midst of the interview, he cautioned of the computer's limits and tendencies to frustrate its creative user. The computer's written program, he said, "won't let you create new words."

Today, the more advanced computer seems more lenient. It may question a new word with a scraggly red underline. But it will let you keep the word if you want it.

You'll also need to battle that tendency with conservative editors. An insightful editor will see where you're going as you creatively stray. A caring editor, if not understanding it, will discuss it with you. Fearful editors will try to limit you. Don't let them. Continue to trust that loving, intelligent energy—the Muse. Continue to go deep, and take chances. Oh, and this especially: Continue to thank the Muse after you have collaborated.

Bless.

I WANT TO DIE LIVING

I want to die living. I want my heart
to explode while dancing, not just hiding
in damp caves from dark beasts. I want to start
now as the sun rises, mind abiding
in prayer, eyes celebrating each found soul
gliding past—fertile pollen for all that's
civilized. Let me inspire, not console,
my psyche's timid wandering, combat
deep fear by laughing at its horrid glare,
calling it outside to join our long run,
forsake its eternal "no". Who knows where
all new trails lead? Love knows we've just begun
our hope's faithful search for new dimensions.
We leap in by choice – our great decision.

Roger Armbrust
June 8, 2016

six suggestions to teachers
Guiding Young Poets and Writers (Those Young in the Work)

1. When students register for, or are assigned, the writing course, instruct them to bring in one typed poem of their own to the first class.

2. First class: Read and discuss personal views of the Muse. Do you believe? How do you define your personal Muse? What are your hopes and dreams?

   Invite them to some quiet time of Free Writing, putting down whatever flows through them.

   Have them turn in the typed poems they brought. Let the students know you will take their first typed poems, read them, write comments, and return them the next class.

3. From here on, students bring in one typed poem each class, with copies for you and other students. Allow at least half of each class period to let three or four students read their poems and receive class responses.

4. Stress FAITHFUL, LOVING criticism: HONESTY with CARE. End each poem's discussion with your summary of the valid criticisms and suggestions. Encourage each poet and writer to continue moving forward.

5. Play audio readings of poetry (famous poets reading their own work, if possible), and ask students to respond to what they've

heard. Do they hear the "music"? What image or images capture them? Can they apply the poem somehow to their own experience, imagination, and dreams?

6. Ask these same questions, and your own, regarding the students' poems when they read them aloud. Also, when coming up with your own questions: Go Deep, Take Chances.

Referenced Works

p. 13

Akhmatova, A. (1990). "The Muse". *The complete poems of Anna Akhmatova*. Somerville, MA. Zephyr Press.

pp. 15

James, W. (2004). *The varieties of religious experience*. New York. Barnes and Noble Classics (Wayne Proudfoot, intro.)

p. 16

Goethe, J. (1870). *Faust*. Boston. Houghton Mifflen.

p. 17

Bloom, H. (2004). *Where shall wisdom be found?* New York. Riverhead Books (Penguin Group)

p. 21

Williams, M. (1989). "Let Me Tell You". *Living on the surface: new and selected poems*. Baton Rouge, LA. Louisiana State University Press.

p. 24

Joyce, J. (1916). A portrait of the artist as a young man. New York. B.W. Huebsch.

p. 24

Wolfe, T. (1929). *Look homeward angel*. New York. Charles Scribner's Sons.

p. 24

Yeats, W. (1917). "Broken Dreams". *The wild swans at coole*. Dublin. Cuala Press.

p. 27

James, W. (1896). *Is life worth living?* Philadelphia. International Journal of Ethics: University of Chicago Press.

p. 30, 37

Whitman, W. (1892). *Leaves of grass*. Philadelphia. David McKay Publications

p. 42
Stevens, W. (1923). "Sunday Morning", *Harmonium*. New York. Alfred A. Knopf

p. 55
Sherrill, J. (1955) "Robert Frost and Faith", *Guideposts*. Harlan, IA.

p. 56
Frost, R. (1923) "The Star-Splitter", *New Hampshire*. New York. Henry Holt and Company

p. 56
Rilke, R. (1905). *The book of hours*. Leipzig, Germany. Insel Verlag

p. 57
Rilke, R. (1929). *Letters to a young poet*. (tr. Herter Norton, 1993). New York. W.W. Norton & Company

p. 106
Auden, W. (1939). "Voltaire at Ferney". Chicago Poetry: A Magazine of Verse

p. 119
Packard, W. (1992) *The art of poetry writing*. New York. St. Martin's Press

For further reading, point your browser to:

www.parkhurstbrothers.com

CPSIA information can be obtained
at www.ICGtesting.com
Printed in the USA
JSHW011558090220
4073JS00002B/65

9 781624 910906